CW01667595

PORTOBELLO HOUSING CO-OPERATIVE

THE FIRST FORTY YEARS

Written by
Michael O'Dwyer

Grosvenor House
Publishing Limited

This book is published by
Grosvenor House Publishing Ltd
Link House
140 The Broadway, Tolworth, Surrey, KT6 7HT.
www.grosvenorhousepublishing.co.uk

A CIP record for this book
is available from the British Library

Portobello Housing Co-operative Ltd. Registered Address, 79, Tavistock Road, London W11 1AR.

ISBN 978-1-78623-340-0

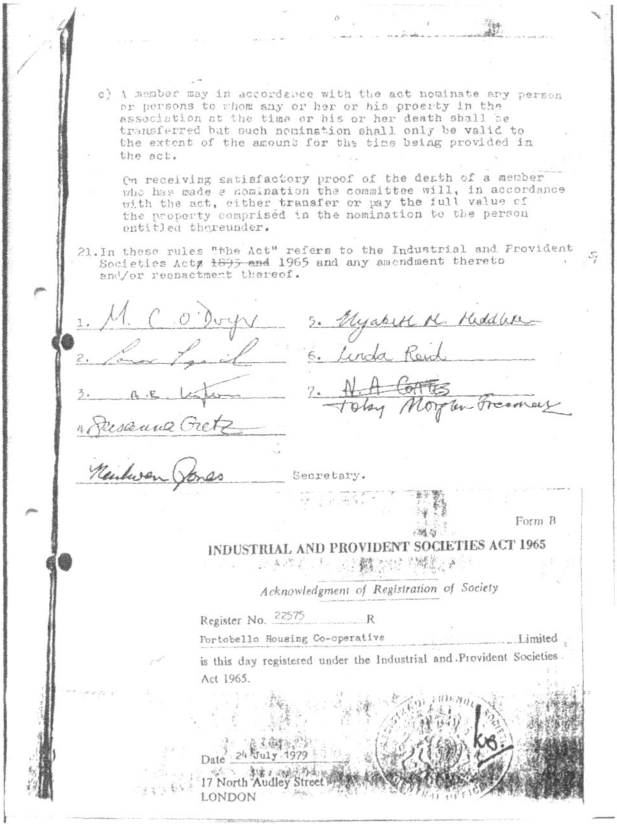

c) A member may in accordance with the act nominate any person or persons to whom any or her or his proerty in the association at the time or his or her death shall be transferred but such nomination shall only be valid to the extent of the amount for the time being provided in the act.

On receiving satisfactory proof of the death of a member who has made a nomination the committee will, in accordance with the act, either transfer or pay the full value of the property comprised in the nomination to the person entitled thereunder.

21. In these rules "the Act" refers to the Industrial and Provident Societies Act~~s 1893 and~~ 1965 and any amendment thereto and/or reonactment thereof.

1. M. C. O'Dwyer
2.
3. A. B.
4. Susanna Gretz
5. Elizabeth M. Middleton
6. Linda Reid
7. ~~N. A. Coates~~ Toby Morgan-Freeman

Secretary.

Form B

INDUSTRIAL AND PROVIDENT SOCIETIES ACT 1965

Acknowledgment of Registration of Society

Register No. 22575 R

Portobello Housing Co-operative Limited

is this day registered under the Industrial and Provident Societies Act 1965.

Date 24 July 1979

17 North Audley Street
LONDON

1. Founders and Incorporation (1979)

Author's Note

Mike was born in Manchester, in 1951, to Irish parents. He read Law in Liverpool in the early '70s followed by a year volunteering in a local community law centre. He moved to London in 1976, joining one of the few legal aid firms and completed his traineeship two years later. Arriving in North Kensington in 1978 to take up a post as housing solicitor with the local Law Centre he joined with others to found the Portobello Housing Co-operative that year. Throughout the 1980s, Mike was a pioneer in establishing housing law rights for tenants and the homeless through a series of campaigns, going on to work in similar fashion in a number of other London Boroughs for several decades, until his retirement in 2015. He continues to use his legal skills within the National Health Service and for local charities. He has lived in Co-op property, in North Kensington, for over 35 years.

Acknowledgements

The PHC History Project began in 2016 with a recognition that many ex-members had worked tirelessly to initially form and later develop the organisation which exists today. To acknowledge this heritage, it was decided to commission the author to write this history. To guide the work, it was decided to establish an editorial group, comprising not only past and present members but also members of the community of North Kensington. Accountability lay directly to the Co-op's General Meeting with regular reports during the project. Thanks goes to all those who agreed to be interviewed for the publication and to all members of the editorial group, in particular to Sean Canning who carried out the editing.

CONTENTS

Key to illustrations

PREFACE

Housing in North Kensington 1950 – 1980

Like many other parts of London, North Kensington suffered from bomb damage in the Second World War, resulting in a mixture of properties being destroyed or damaged. In the late '40s, as there was a shortage of money around, private individuals spent very little in restoring the properties and many were snapped up by private landlords to rent out. The local authority, in contrast to others in the capital, did not at that time intervene with clearance programmes and so conditions deteriorated.

This was graphically illustrated by Alan Johnson in the first part of his autobiography, "This Boy" (Bantam Press, 2015) describing the housing conditions he experienced as a very young boy growing up in the early 1950's:

"We lived, courtesy of the Rowe Housing Trust, at 107, Southam Street, North Kensington, London W10 – a street whose buildings had been condemned in the 1930s. At least one family occupied each of the four floors and the dank basement. Before my arrival Lily, Steve and Linda had lived in one room but when I was born they had given us two rooms on a higher floor, one for sleeping in and one for eating in. Everyone used the same front door and the single decrepit toilet in the small concrete yard that backed on to the railway line in and out of Paddington Station. There was no electricity in the house – or outside for that matter".(Johnson, page 12)

Again, "With no fridge and the buckets of urine in the bedroom (to avoid having to go out into the yard in the middle of the night) our house was a more attractive venue for the discerning fly than it was for us. There were cockroaches, beetles and all manner of bugs." (Johnson, page.16)

The nature of the properties in W10 and W11 (mainly large, multi-storeyed mid to late Victorian terraced houses) were ideal to be broken up into "bed-sits" (comprising bedroom, living room and kitchen together) along with one-bedroom units - thus providing low cost accommodation. The previous decade had seen many immigrants from the Caribbean settle in the area, attracted by the prospects of work in the capital but inevitably earning only low incomes. North Kensington provided affordable housing and the area became attractive to private landlords, the most notorious of whom was Peter Rachman. By the mid 1950's, Rachman was buying property across W11, including Powis Terrace (Hedgegate Court), Powis Square, Powis Gardens, Colville Road and Colville Terrace. In terms of landlord and tenant relations, there was almost no policing by the local authority and in 1957, the Government introduced the disastrous 1957 Rent Act, which swept away any rent control and stripped tenants of any security from eviction.

Alan Johnson (in his biography referred to above) provides this contemporary account of the Colville district, "At that time new tenants did not have the same protection as sitting tenants and people coming from the West Indies in response to the call for workers in Britain, found it almost impossible to find a place to live. They had no alternative but to accept poor conditions and extortionate rents while Rachman placed as many of them as he could into shared accommodation, by subdividing houses in to multiple small rooms." (Johnson, page.48)

By the late 1950's the immigrant community in Notting Hill (that is; including North Kensington and spreading down to Notting Hill Gate) was estimated to be around 7,000 but there was resentment from parts of the white community. In 1958 a gang of white rioters surged out of Notting Dale (an adjacent area), over Ladbroke Grove and into the Colville district (described in the previous paragraph). Much damage was done and violence continued for several months until in May 1959, a young black youth, Kelso Cochrane was stabbed and killed on Golborne Road W10. At his funeral, it was estimated that more than 1,200 people followed the hearse in procession up Ladbroke Grove, from St. Michael's Church to Kensal Cemetery. This was the first recognised statement against racism by the black community- a few short years later processions began which have turned into what is now the "Notting Hill Carnival". It is not without significance that part of the Carnival route today covers that taken in 1959.

Conditions in the privately rented sector continued to deteriorate in the early '60s, with many reports of inhuman living conditions, "harassment" (landlord interference) and evictions. This reached national prominence in 1963-64 when, following a salacious sex scandal (the Profumo Affair) involving a government minister, John Profumo, the notorious landlord Peter Rachman and a femme fatale, Christine Keeler, the appalling conditions of Rachman's properties and those forced to live in them came to public attention. The Prime Minster (Harold Macmillan) took some immediate action (which didn't prevent him losing power in 1965). As the scandal of living conditions was emerging, the Housing Act 1964 was introduced - though largely ineffective and ill-thought out. Eventually, Sir Milner Holland was asked to report on housing conditions in Greater London. The release of the report, in 1965, led to the Protection from Eviction Act of that year, making it a criminal act to unlawfully interfere with or evict, a tenant, whilst the Rent Act of 1965 re-established some rent control and introduced some security against eviction for "unfurnished" tenants (though not for "furnished" tenants).

The Milner Holland report had identified that there was a shortage of rented accommodation in London, which itself had been recognised by a group of community activists and church leaders in Notting Hill, at least since the race riots of the late '50s. They resolved to carry on, into a new era, the work of the established local housing trusts, such as Kensington, Octavia Hill, Peabody etc. and in Blenheim Crescent W11, in 1963, they formed the Notting Hill Housing Trust. The initial years were modest with purchases coming through charitable donations and refurbishment waiting until further funds became available.

Meanwhile, the community in North Kensington and Notting Hill had begun to come together and in1967 it really took off. Early in 1967 there was the collapse of a property company in Notting Hill which had a reputation for slum lettings. A meeting of over 300 angry tenants resolved to set up an organisation to resist any evictions and to protect their rights. They formed themselves into the, "Notting Hill People's Association" which later that year organised a survey of house conditions, it began lobbying the local authority to get involved. One of the outcomes of their activity was the establishment of the Housing Action Centre to provide assistance to residents; it lasted for over 30 years. Finally, in 1969, the Department of the Environment began to ask questions of the Council, which responded, through a new leader, with some radical thinking. It recognised that, retrospectively, it needed to intervene to tackle sub-standard conditions on an area basis, in order to preserve the character of the local community and also that Housing Trusts (known more commonly now as, "Housing Associations") needed subsidies in order to both buy properties at a market rate and refurbish them. Both initiatives were completely novel.

On the 28th July 1970, the Minister for the Environment, Michael Heseltine, proclaimed the "Western Avenue Extension" open. An elevated, concrete, multi-laned highway running through the heart of North Kensington (known now as the "Westway") had caused the demolition of hundreds of properties but had left some units in Walmer and Acklam Roads within feet of what was to be a major trunk route. The residents discovered a route on to the new motorway via a slip-road at Paddington Station and the cavalcade confronted the Minister during his television interviews on site. It took further confrontations and another invasion of the Westway, for the argument for demolition and re-housing to be won.

Less than 10 days before the Motorway incident, the first Law Centre in the U.K., had opened its doors in a former butcher's shop in Golborne Road W10. North Kensington Law Centre was started by one solicitor and two others as a result for the need identified by the Peoples' Association and others. It was designed to be community led and not-for-profit, without hierarchies. A good example of the need for its services was taking place within feet of its doorstep. In May 1970, tenants in St. Ervan's Road W10 suffered extreme harassment. Whilst out, the landlord had boarded up the front door, hired a furniture van and told them to move to Wandsworth. After intervention, a meeting of residents on the Road called for the Council to take over the property. A month later the landlord took the front door off and locked it in the basement leaving three families unprotected. In the absence of Council action, the tenants turned to the new Law Centre which conducted a private prosecution against the landlord, resulting in an award of damages.

Following the change of practice by the Council, in 1969, Housing Association (HA) activity had continued steadily within financial constraints but this was to change with the passing of the Housing Act 1974. This recognised much of what had been happening at the local level in Kensington, but brought with it, extra finance. In addition to grants for purchase (Housing Association Grants) the shortfall between fair rents and the cost of purchase/refurbishment was recognised by the introduction of "Revenue Deficit Grant" for HAs and "Housing Action Areas" were established with enhanced powers for Councils to enforce improvement of standards. The first Action Area was declared in the Colville/Tavistock (W11) area of North Kensington, Notting Hill Housing Trust was given special zoned interest and one of the detailed provisions was that any landlord seeking to dispose of a rented property had to offer it first to an Association. Accordingly, it is estimated that Associations bought or improved approximately 5,000 dwellings in North Kensington in the 15 years to 1982.

Following the groundbreaking legislation on housing standards in 1974, 1977 saw a spate of legislation aimed at the rights of the occupier in privately rented accommodation. The Rent Act 1977 introduced, "protected tenancies" to be the default status (which brought in restricted grounds for possession) and "fair rents, set by an independent rent officer. Landlords immediately set about constructing artificial "sham" lettings (it would take the law most of a decade to correct this – see later). To help prevent unlawful, often violent, evictions by landlords seeking vacant possession to profit from sale, the Protection from Eviction Act was amended in 1977 to shift the burden of proof and increase penalties. Further, in an attempt to provide a structure to assist those with absolutely nowhere to live (most vividly highlighted in the documentary, "Cathy Come Home" a decade earlier) a duty was placed on local authorities to provide accommodation to the most vulnerable through the Housing (Homeless Persons) Act 1977. Noticeably, most single people were excluded from any right to housing.

Two years later a Conservative government was elected, led by Prime Minister, Margaret Thatcher. She had a fixed ideology which promoted the privatisation of council housing and the introduction of market-based solutions, in a determined effort to end municipalisation (but in favour of self-help); almost immediately it resulted in passing the 1980 Housing Act with the introduction of the "right to buy" Council property (without plans to replace social housing stock). This practice was to have a devastating effect on housing supply in London, a major result being an increase in the number of homeless households living in temporary accommodation from below 1,000 in 1980, to 8,000 in 1987.

"Squatting" is an ancient expression, mainly used to describe the process of someone occupying land (or in this case, property for rent) which doesn't belong to them. By the end of the '70s, there were tens of thousands of people occupying unused or abandoned buildings across London. The number of vacant properties had increased due to a variety of factors including disrepair; clearance areas; lack of money to convert - the various reasons would reflect the nature of the area. Therefore, in areas with large local authority owned stock, the majority of squatting would be in those properties. In North Kensington the proportion of Council housing was low, but following the rise of the Housing Trusts, there were increasing numbers of vacant properties where the sitting tenants had been re-housed but the fabric not touched due to lack of resources. Thus squatting in housing association properties was big locally. It was always easy for landlords to remove squatters through the "Summary Procedure" which was swift and put the burden of proof on the occupier to show how they had a right to reside.

It was, no doubt, those pressures which lead to a group of squatters from different parts of North Kensington, to meet in a community centre on Kensington Park Road W11 in July 1976 and to resolve to set up a group to look for housing.

It named itself, West Eleven Housing Co-operative (W.11 Coop) and whereas its individual members had separate housing experiences, they bound together to provide a unified face and resolved not to make a profit out of the provision of housing. After making contacts and showing that it was a reliable entity, it entered into a management agreement with Notting Hill Housing Trust for a property at 32, Lancaster Road, W11. The Co-op would house some of its members; pay rent to the Trust and ensure the upkeep of the building. The Trust would receive a modest allowance from the Government (for a, "special project") and the property would remain vacant until enough money was available to convert it. Within 10 years the Co-op would have retained the initial building and had gained a total of 10 further properties in the cluster between Lancaster Road and All Saints Road, W11. Word spread rapidly amongst single people locally who were residing in sub standard accommodation and interest in the Co-op began to increase.

There was also an interest in collective action providing results. At the west end of North Kensington there is a triangle of land wedged between the back of Latimer Road Tube Station and the "West Cross Route" (M40 feeder road), it includes Freston Road and it traverses W10 and W11. Since the beginning of the 1970's, the Greater London Council (GLC) had abandoned the area after re-housing its tenants. In the absence of occupiers, these properties became squatted to the extent that by 1973 there were approximately 120 residents. Eventually the G.L.C. got around to forming plans for redevelopment but the residents, in true theatrical style, held a referendum which declared the area *"the People's Republic of Frestonia"*, resolved to join the European Union and petitioned the United Nations for help to avoid being "invaded" (in October 1977). The area rapidly became one of the most vibrant centres for performing arts in London and gained an international reputation. In the mid 1980's, after the abolition of the GLC, Notting Hill Housing Trust acquired large tracts of the area and (no doubt as a result of their experience with other Co-ops in North Kensington) agreed that the ex-squatters could remain as Co-op members managing their properties. This continues today.

PART 1

THE EARLY YEARS 1980 to 1990

Formation

In the mid to late 1970s, living conditions for most single people in Notting Hill (as in the rest of London) were difficult. There was a shortage of accommodation; most tenancies provided little security and little action was taken by the local authority to challenge appalling conditions. The homeless safety net did not stretch to singles. Some of those who would go on to establish Portobello Housing Co-operative, describe their living conditions in 1978, as follows:

"I had to move to 182, Ladbroke Grove W11, a dilapidated building with 5 stories and a basement (where an old guy lived without electricity). Above the first floor was completely uninhabitable." (Linda Reid)

"I occupied a flat at 35, Bassett Road W10 but there was no heat and the bath was in the hall." (Susie Gretz)

"I was sharing in Talbot Road W11, there were no front doors to people's places and no bathroom (we would wash in the sink). There was no re-housing for single people." (Alison Sage)

"I was living with my partner in W10. We had a Greek landlady who lived downstairs. She went back to Greece and the property was sold to developers who wanted us out" (Rob Small)

One name is commonly mentioned by those who were there at the beginning – Anna Malcolm. Anna was a seasoned Scot who had worked at the Law Centre throughout the '70s on housing issues and who had been consulted by many single people in housing need. She was also a founder member of W11 Housing Co-operative, itself often a suggestion to the young local homeless as a possible solution to housing problems.

Unfortunately when prospective members approached the W11 Co-op, they found it had been inundated with enquiries and was more than full. The consensus was that it could be possible to start a new Co-op, which might itself attract housing solutions. Fortunately, one of the most experienced members of W11, Jason Copeland, agreed to give a new group the benefit of his experience in setting up Co-ops. As a result, in or around October 1978, a group began to meet in Liz Middleton's flat in Norland Square W11. Meetings would shift from place to place, mostly hosted by interested individuals in their flats and bed-sits, but also, sometimes in local meeting places, including one sunken venue under the Motorway (at 1, Thorpe Close W10) known as, "The Pit".

Up the road was the local music venue, Acklam Hall, where a number of the initial participants of the fledgling Co-op went to a "Rock against Racism" gig in June 1979. The concert was attacked by far right militants and extensive damage was caused, an example of local volatility in the post punk-rock era. The consensus emerged amongst attendees that everyone wanted to tackle housing problems collectively, without seeking a profit and as part of the community of North Kensington. In recognition of the traditional common lane which runs through the area the name of "Portobello Housing Co-operative" was chosen. It was immediately recognised that a formal legal structure was needed and Mike O'Dwyer, a member of the group and newly qualified housing solicitor at the Law Centre was delegated to work with Jason Copeland, on the detail. However, it was also recognised that money for running costs would be needed.

Self Help and Fundraising

After the completion of the Westway motorway, the North Kensington Amenity Trust was formed to preserve and promote the land under the flyover for the benefit of the local community. This was deeply controversial, both in its remit and the composition of its governance, but also in its methodology in the maximisation of commercial over community development (these themes continue today). The centrepiece at the end of the '70s was the market area under the canopy at the junction of Portobello and Oxford Gardens, this is where "community stalls" were allocated on a Saturday (the peak market day). At the start of 1979, those growing the Co-op decided it would be useful to have a visible presence on the Road from which it was taking its name and also maybe make some start-up money.

Rob Small recounts:

"We had a rota and everyone was paired off. On Saturday morning you had to be there by 6am and check in with the market manager, then wait. After the commercial stalls had been allocated, we would get ours. I had a Renault 4 and used to run around in the week to collect things from all over, they would be stashed in someone's flat. I remember, it was freezing in winter"

Alison Sage remembers:

"We went round in two's, anywhere at random. We knocked on doors and were given jumble by hand."

Not everyone enjoyed the experience, Tony Layton describes:

"Most of what we had on offer was rubbish. We had to stay there all day, often freezing, and only make about £20."

The stall would go on to last for more than two years and despite bringing in a small but steady income, ready cash was needed, so in the spring of 1979, someone had the bright idea of having a Jumble Sale. Premises were secured for a Saturday at Portobello Court, on the junction of Portobello Road and Westbourne Park Road, right in the middle of the market. Much of the stall stock was used but feelers were put out further afield too. Susie Gretz recalls "I remember receiving posh calls from Belgravia" and Tony Layton adds "we got stuff from a Countess". By all accounts, the day was a great success. Tony Layton remembers that "there was a huge queue outside. "When we opened it was pandemonium, people were pushing each other out of the way. Later, we sent one of us outside in a Top Hat to call more in." Those present estimate that about £400 was taken, enough to provide for initial running costs.

2. Outside the First Property (1987)

Rules and Regulations

On the 24th July 1979, the Co-op was registered as an "Industrial & Provident Society", established under the 1965 Act. This provided a legal structure very much like that of a Limited Company (though not-for-profit). The members were to contribute £1 for one share and in the event of dissolution that would be the share capital. The governing instrument, which had been approved on registration, was known as "The Rules" and subscribed by seven of the group who had been meeting in the months before.

The fundamental purpose of the organisation was described thus:

- "The construction, conversion, improvement and management, on the co-operative principle, of houses (and land) for occupation by members of the association under an agreement made between each member and the association."

Some of the other vital clauses included:

- The registered office, established at 74, Golborne Road, W10 (the Law Centre;. Crucially, only members would be able to occupy its property (known in jargon as "fully mutual"); All management required decisions to be taken in the General Meeting (GM) of all members, which would be the supreme power, with the duty to make binding decisions on behalf of the whole Co-op; There would have to be a GM at least every month (in fact the Co-op has met on a Friday evening, bi-weekly, since that time) and everyone would be expected to attend.
- There was provision for an Annual General Meeting (AGM); yearly accounts which were to be audited; for

reports to the Registrar and for the election of officers, initially the Chairperson, Treasurer and Secretary.

Apart from two amendments, the same Rules remain in place today.

After registration, the Co-op set about to create its governance arrangements and a large number of "Standing Orders" were passed in 1979 in order to provide for a proper working structure. These included;

- Any property allocation would be based on the housing need of members and their commitment to the Co-op;
- Membership of the Co-op would be limited to 30 in order to maximise participation and ensure responsibility in matters such as payment of rent;
- Protection of finances through establishment of a sub-committee (everyone was to be allocated to a particular sub-committee);
- Everyone was to receive minutes of each GM but would risk losing membership if missing more than 4 meetings without apologies.

Many more regulations would be passed later as we shall see, but for the moment, at the beginning of 1980, the Co-op was ready for action.

Development and Occupation of Property (1)

A Conservative Government had been elected in1979 and Margaret Thatcher had taken post as Prime Minister. At first there were mixed thoughts about the implications for Portobello Housing Co-operative (PHC). Whilst it was recognised that Mrs. Thatcher was in favour of an agenda based on market-based solutions and privatisation and against, "municipalisation"; the housing association lobby was strong (Notting Hill Housing Trust (NHHT) had around 2,000 dwellings in Kensington by this time) and was likely to expand. For PHC, self-help and tenant empowerment was seen as something good to strive for. Nationally, the bombshell was the passing of the Housing Act 1980 which brought with it the "Right to Buy" Council property. The cumulative effect of the loss of public sector stock (5 million units lost in the first 5 years alone) would have a negative impact on re-housing for homeless households up to and including the present day. However, the fact that it would be several years before housing associations were required to lose stock, meant that in North Kensington a variety of tenures continued, contributing to the area's unique identity.

One of the first decisions PHC had made was that it would hold out for the collective ownership of property, rather than to be a vehicle for the long-term management of units owned by another housing association. However, realistically, the process of acquisition and development was extremely complex, needing much more infrastructure than the Co-op was ever likely to have. The Co-op needed a development agent and it turned to the second largest housing association in the area, the Kensington Housing Trust (KHT). Very much like the connection between NHHT and W11 housing co-operative; KHT was interested in working with a "special project" such as PHC and agreed to be its development agent (in principal - because PHC still had various hoops to get through).

Almost immediately, in 1980, the Department of the Environment declared a moratorium on new spending for housing associations whilst the future direction of policy was worked out. Following the moratorium, KHT found itself with properties which it had bought but had no finance to convert and improve, having re-housed any sitting tenants. It asked PHC if it could help by occupying some of its empty property, on short term licences (known as "short-life"). The advantages to both sides were apparent - KHT would have "caretakers" covering expenditure such as "rates" (now council tax) and modest management charges, preventing further deterioration of the property and would avoid problems such as having to evict squatters when possession was needed. For PHC, we have seen that its members were in housing need and subject to bad landlordism. Without having to commit to become a long-term management agency, PHC could use its experience as a landlord in short-life to show how it would operate once it owned property. The Co-op members were also prepared to put voluntary effort into run-down units with no prospect of long-term housing. Many had experience of doing just that in squats and rented accommodation.

Accordingly, in 1981, the Co-op occupied 3 units in 2 properties. By 1982 that had risen to 5 properties housing 16 members; by 1983 this had increased to 6 properties housing 21 members and by1986 there were a total of 8 properties housing 23 members. Properties were always handed back on time, with no disputes. The Co-op was charged a licence fee by the Trust and it passed that on (with a small management charge) to the occupying member, by way of a written licence agreement.

Horror and Housing Litigation

25-27-29, Clanricarde Gardens in Notting Hill Gate were a series of large Victorian terraced properties which had been converted into numerous bed-sits occupied mainly by migrant workers employed in nearby hotels and restaurants. The properties were owned by a landlord, "Charlie" Pouyiouros whose track record was so bad that he had a number of properties confiscated by an adjoining Council due to neglect of tenant's welfare and failure to repair.

On the night of the 15th December 1981, all three houses were destroyed by fire. Almost 100 people were made homeless as a result of the tragedy which claimed eight lives. Many people were detained in hospital with resulting injuries; 34 people were rescued from window ledges and 12 escaped down drainpipes or by knotting sheets. A senior fire officer at the scene observed that the death toll could easily have been much higher. It emerged that the houses were packed with people paying high rents. The maze of corridors provided a perfect tunnel for the fire to spread, the fire precautions were faulty and in most areas, non-existent. The properties were a fire trap without any real means of escape.

The author, at the Law Centre, was inundated by both the bereaved and by survivors looking for justice. Rapid preparations were made for representation at the Inquest, which investigated the tragic deaths. Over two weeks, next of kin and ex-occupants argued that the landlord was effectively guilty of manslaughter but in the end the jury left the question open. The horrific events became a catalyst for the housing aid movement and an organisation called the Campaign for Bed-sit Rights was formed. A piece of legislation entitled the Houses in Multiple Occupation (HMOs) Bill was promoted and sponsored in Parliament by a backbencher. Its core provisions were:

- Any owner of these dwellings would be under a duty to safeguard the health and safety of tenants with a right of redress through the Courts;
- Local Authorities were required to enforce proper standards and re-house those made homeless as a result;
- Owners of HMOs were required to register with the local authority. Councils to be given powers to close down properties, which failed to comply with minimum standards.

The Bill was presented in February 1982 and received a second reading, with well over one hundred M.P.s supporting it, however it failed to reach the statue book in time before the Thatcher government called the 1983 general election and fell accordingly.

The Inquest into the deaths at Clanricarde Gardens threw up some alarming information. In the years before the fire there had been a stream of complaints to the Town Hall about conditions in the properties which had been previously inspected by fire officers in 1980, who confirmed that they were dangerous for occupants. A formal complaint was made to the Local Government Ombudsman and his report was issued in October 1983. It found that the Council's delay in carrying out full inspections constituted maladministration, yet, with twisted logic it also found that the landlord would not have been required to comply with any enforcement by the time of the fire.

Time Out — May 1982

Behind The Bedsitterland Fire

West London flats go up in flames, shouts ignored, doors locked. SUE BALDING reports on the horrific fire that killed eight people last December, and its aftermath.

One night last December more than 100 people were crammed into the 56-bedsit rabbit warren that had been made out of three houses in Clanricarde Gardens, Notting Hill. A fire started.

Several people ignored shouts from neighbours because they feared a fight outside. Instead they locked their doors. Eight people died.

Last Friday the inquest into that fire ended with a verdict of misadventure. Barristers representing relatives of the dead had urged the jury to return an 'unlawful killing' verdict, they argued that the landlord had a 'duty to care' towards his tenants.

One thing has come out of the fire. The Paddington and North Kensington Law Centres, Shelter, Shac and tenants' organisations are pushing for tougher action by local authorities and for stricter laws on fire safety.

Tenants told the inquest of lights that continually fused, of electric meters that sparked when fed with coins, of a ceiling that had collapsed. Fire and electricity board experts described the dangerous wiring, and the lack of fire precautions.

The occupants were elderly, single people, childless couples and South American and Spanish service workers for the West End's hotel industry.

Tragedies like the Clanricarde Gardens fire, and the increasing pressure on the private market, seem to be changing things. Paddington Federation of Tenants and Residents Associations and the Camden Federation of Private Tenants are two organisations supporting tenants of private landlords.

While the market continues to shrink, conditions continue to worsen. The Greater London Council's House Condition survey found that one third of homes unfit were owned by private landlords. And the amount of rented housing shrunk from 24.1% in 1966 to 13.9% in 1978.

Rent Act evasions are now widespread, with most new lettings consisting of licences, holiday lets and

Clanricarde Gardens after the fire and landlord Charambasias Ponyiouros (inset).

The ghost of Peter Rachman, the 1960s slum king, lives on in West London where, in the same area that gained such notoriety 20 years ago, tenants are experiencing increasing harassment as they stand in the way of profitable conversions. The recent Select Committee into the private rented sector were told by the Paddington Federation that conditions were now worse than in the Rachman era, since the most profit-

version for sale on long leases. An added bonus to potential speculators, they point out, is the availability in Westminster of improvement grants, on which in many parts of the borough no conditions are imposed to guarantee future lettings.

Last year the Paddington Law Centre applied for 39 injunctions to protect tenants from harassment, compared to two or three in previous years.

Eight people died and 100 were made homeless when fire swept through this Notting Hill bedsit block in December 1981.
Photo: Manchester Evening News

3. Bedsitterland fire (1982-1984)

Left without any means of redress, some fire survivors returned to the Law Centre and instructed lawyers to take action against the landlord. Early in 1984, 13 ex-tenants commenced High Court legal proceedings alleging that the landlord, Mr. Pouyiouros had been guilty of negligence in failing to have ensured proper measures to contain the fire; nor provide any means of escape - leading to loss of lives, health and property. So began a long search for justice.

Housing Pressure in North Kensington

Elsewhere in the area it was clear that different groups were also having major housing problems. For instance for travellers, who had traditionally settled in an area of W10 known as Notting Dale since the late1800s. In 1975 they were accommodated on an official site, located under the M40 adjacent to Latimer Road, designated jointly by both Hammersmith & Fulham and Kensington and Chelsea. The site was too small for demand (by then the community comprised Irish travellers) with inadequate plumbing, lighting and other facilities making the location dangerous. The Law Centre was instructed to conduct a criminal prosecution over conditions, resulting in convictions against both Councils in 1982. Immediately plans were drawn up by both Councils, to close the site and eject families (including over a hundred children). A representative of the families, Martin Ward, instructed the Law Centre Housing Unit, on behalf of the site residents, to help save the site. The Government (Secretary of State for the Environment) refused to intervene and when plans were made to cut off the water supply and the electricity, urgent action was started in the High Court including the issue of an injunction. In October 1983, after a week-long hearing with Q.C.s representing the two Councils, the Government, the Amenity Trust and even the GLC, Mr. Justice Woolf ruled that the site had to be provided and there could be no interference with occupation facilities. It was the first time an individual traveller had ever brought such an action against the public authorities. Although arguments have continued over its sufficiency and location over the years, it remains open today and is still the only official site for travellers in West London.

Elsewhere in the area, other tenants were having an equally horrific time. Lancaster West was (and is) the largest Council estate locally, with 960 flats housing up to 3,000 people. Since 1981 it had experienced a saturation infestation of cockroaches. One person reported insects dropping off the ceiling at tea time, another of finding them in the baby's cot, or of waking up to brush them from bedclothes at night. Cockroaches were spotted in radios and even fridges! The estate had a common heating system and the insects found an ideal breeding found in void areas including heating ducts in common parts and inside the flats.

Despite constant complaints, the Council had no, "block control treatment" (where all flats in a locality are treated at the same time) and matters just got worse, leading to a petition by 230 tenants which was ignored by the Council. To compound matters, treatment to the heating ducts involved workers drilling through the fabric which turned out to be dangerous asbestos, resulting in the release of airborne fibres into the domestic environment. Eventually a specialist firm was brought in to carry out the work properly. After being refused compensation, the tenants again turned to the Law Centre Housing Unit and legal proceedings for negligence were brought against the Council. After a long trial, in October 1985, Judge Honig at Central London County Court found the Council had breached their duty of care to the tenants. Matters cited included late and defective treatment, use of the wrong chemicals and a failure to monitor the results. The family bringing the action were awarded compensation and legal costs. After the trial the

Council initially refused to compensate any other tenants but after a year-long campaign it climbed down and the final bill was estimated to be about £750,000. Unfortunately, by the time of the trial, not enough research had been done within the United Kingdom into the effect of released airborne asbestos fibres in the domestic environment and so that had to be left to be fought on another day.

Kensington News

A LONDON NEWSPAPER GROUP PUBLICATION   EST 1869   KN 1129   Thursday, April 26, 1990   TEL: 081-741 1622   25p

IN BRIEF

Hold on to your purse

NOTTING Hill police are warning people who visit Portobello Road market on Saturdays to be extra careful with their wallets and purses after a spate of pickpocketing.

There has been a marked increase which police believe is due to "dippers" returning to the market for the summer.

Museum jobs to go

THE Natural History Museum announced the loss of 100 jobs on Monday as part of a new corporate plan to make its finances more business-like. It hopes most of the cuts will be achieved through natural wastage and voluntary redundancies.

Night raid

ANTIQUES and silver worth £25,000 were stolen from a house in Kensington Gate between Friday evening and Saturday morning.

Terrified family lives in 'hell'

COCKROACH NIGHTMARE

by FIONA CAMERON

A PLAGUE of giant cockroaches has gripped a North Kensington council estate five years after tenants successfully sued the Royal Borough over a similar outbreak.

Toraya Ghailne, of Upper Clarendon Walk, described her horror as she woke up to find the huge, black vermin crawling up her legs.

Mrs Ghailne, who is four months pregnant, said: "I just screamed and screamed. I felt so dirty. At night there are literally hundreds of them and my children are afraid to go to sleep."

The Ghailne family have complained to the council about the problem since they moved in five years ago: "A Rentokil man comes to spray every few weeks but they just keep coming back. It is not working and we just want to get out of this hell."

In 1985 North Kensington Law Centre brought a successful test case after a similar infestation left the estate "crawling with cockroaches". The council was forced to pay more than £350,000 compensation to tenants.

Mike O'Dwyer, the solicitor who led the fight at the time, remembers the scale of the problem: "In 1983 there were carpets of them. Cockroaches were dropping off the ceiling on to peoples' plates.

"The council were forced to pay damages after a court found it guilty of negligence by not calling in Rentokil earlier."

Housing chief Robert Orr-Ewing admitted the situation was bad and said housing officers believed Mrs Ghailne's flat to be at the centre of the current outbreak.

He said: "We are aware of the problem and we have put Rentokil in charge. They are the experts. They will be doing a blitz on that whole block and if they recommend we remove and replace infested furniture we will do."

Critics say these are short-term measures and the estate, which is built on the site of an old brewery, will always be prone to pestilence.

Ward councillor Ben Bousquet promised to help Mrs Ghailne fight for compensation but said the problem will not go away easily.

"They can't seem to get rid of cockroaches on that estate. The only solution is to rehouse everyone there and totally fumigate it block by block."

In the meantime the Ghailnes' four young children share one bedroom with their wheelchair-bound grandmother and are terrified of falling asleep for fear of the roaches.

IN BRIEF

Steals on wheels

TWO young boys playing in Holland Park were robbed by bike-riding bandits on Sunday.

The 12-year-olds were approached by two boys who swore at their victims and followed them to Duchess of Bedford's Walk where they stole their wallets.

Both suspects were about 11 years old and slim, one with an Irish accent, the with a cut on the side of his face.

INSIDE

A MARTIAL arts fanatic from Earl's Court has been sent to a mental hospital for knifing a vagrant to death in a West End street. Full story, page 2.

CONTENTS

Oct 18 1985

DUST PERIL ALLEGED

Ken News

ASBESTOS panels in a North Kensington council estate were drilled by council workmen "with absolutely no precautions," a court heard.

The drilling took place in flats at Camelford Court, Lancaster West Estate, so that insecticide could be squirted through the holes at cockroaches.

The move was made to curb a cockroach

"This can accumulate in the air after relatively small damage to the original material," she said.

The Town Hall, represented by Raymond Sears, QC, is understood to be calling leading asbestos experts as witnesses.

Rentokil cleared the cockroach problem after the council's efforts had failed.

The case is expected to last all week.

4. Cockroach Nightmare (1990)

Back in the private rented sector, the Council had set up a Housing Action Area in and around St. Lawrence Terrace W10 in1978, delegating remedial work to the GLC. After 5 years it was still reporting that almost half of the rented properties were sub-standard. The GLC had carried out its own survey of private renters across London and this reported in1983. It found there was widespread ignorance of any legal rights and that those paying high rents were often those with less protection against eviction. There was widespread harassment, with black people and women suffering most. The poorest were paying above average rents and most lettings were "sham" agreements designed to circumvent the Rent Act protection.

Over in North Kensington, single people were still complaining. In June 1983, a report by "Single Homeless Action in West London" confirmed that singles were forced to live in the most overcrowded, insanitary and expensive accommodation in what was the most densely populated borough in London. Findings included,

- over 70% of the borough population were single or childless couples;
- in 6 years there had been a 72% increase in homelessness applications;
- the average waiting time for a Council bedsit was 26 years;
- Privately rented accommodation had shrunk by 60% in the previous 10 years, yet 40% of the remainder was in need of major repair.

Development and Occupation of Property (2)

Armed with KHT's agreement to be its development agent, PHC started out on the road to gain the necessary consents for the purchase of property. With a legal structure and an ongoing track record in providing accommodation through short-life, a meeting was obtained with the Housing Associations Director at the Council, Mr. Peter Chapman who investigated the running of the Co-op to satisfy itself that PHC had adequate governance systems. After persuading Mr. Chapman that the proposition was viable, he agreed to facilitate a meeting with the then Chair of the Health & Housing Committee Cllr. Richard Walker-Arnott. Further rigorous investigations took place and a positive recommendation was forthcoming to the Committee. After passing financial scrutiny, the appropriate approval, again, in principle, was granted at the end of 1981. Armed with this promise of funding an application was made to the Housing Corporation (the Regulator) for registration as a Housing Association (which was the key to unlocking Housing Association Grant). After further investigations, registration was granted in September 1982. Portobello Housing Co-operative had arrived.

Almost immediately the Co-op was faced with the realities of using public money to buy property on the open market. The amount of property speculation was intense. Then, as now, property prices were amongst the highest in the Country and there was no shortage of those with ready money. Added to that were strict limits on housing association expenditure, set by Government and a lack of any existing internal resources to be able to cushion the blows. Co-op documents at the time record that the most difficult problem of all was the amount of time it took to identify and process potential properties for acquisition. This was because the

Co-op had no employees to do the work. Apart from not having any money to pay for employees, members were committed to self-help and shared the tasks. In total during 1983, 12 properties had been investigated with preliminary legal work and paperwork prepared and submitted to the Council, but each of these were aborted as none came within the initial allocation of £100,000.

Finally, a modest property was identified, near the corner of Portobello Road and Tavistock Road. The appropriate pre-acquisition survey was carried out. Following approval from the Council and the Corporation, contracts were exchanged on the 24th February 1984. There followed a cumbersome bureaucratic tendering process together with housing association grant approval, which ran into another spending moratorium, this time declared by the Council. One thing the Co-op was not short of was members in housing need and so on completion of purchase, it promptly secured the services in the property and granted three of its members permission to occupy under short-term (short life) licences.

Tender approval was obtained and the property handed over to builders in February 1986; KHT acted as development agents and the Co-op appointed its own development officer who acted as conduit for decisions taken by PHC. The Co-op had hoped that the intended occupants would have been able to have a significant input, into the development process but this was curtailed due to financial constraints. The works were completed in November 1986, by which time the first tenants had been allocated and they moved in just before Christmas.

…eria led the opening proces- … Village Fair at the Common- …ek.

…rs and drummers, wearing …querading costume of bells, …th, got the event off to a ringing start.

The fair, which runs until Saturday, brings together musicians from countries all over the world, including Malaya, India, Africa and Trinidad. It also includes workshops, background talks and a music market, and is open from 11.30 am to 10 pm daily.

… plea …ter to …ard

"It will not improve services to the community in North Kensington."

The decision to close the Peter Pan ward had been opposed by St. Charles Hospital children's nurses, local GPs, social workers, teachers and Kensington MP Sir Brandon Rhys Williams, she said.

More than 8,500 people signed a petition against the closure.

The CHC also accused the district of breaking a commitment it had made in 1985 to retain and improve the service at St. Charles.

…abaret wraps

costs £80,000, was paid for by the council. It is made of strengthened PVC-coated polyester.

Up the ladder

THE Kensington High Street Association has re-elected British Home Stores manager Alastair McClelland as its…

Portobello opens door

THE PORTOBELLO Housing Co-op was last week able to officially open its first house.

Although the co-op is eight years old, it has until now only been able to provide short let accommodation in houses awaiting refurbishment.

The house, newly refurbished at a cost of £150,000, is at 79 Tavistock Road, North Kensington.

"We hope to continue buying properties for and developing them for the benefit of our members," said founder member Mike O'Dwyer.

The organisation, which is the first housing co-operative to receive funding from Kensington and Chelsea council, specialises in housing for single, homeless people.

"Most of the people on our list are waiting for bedsit accommodation," said Mr O'Dwyer.

The new house contains one family flat and two bedsits.

According to council figures there are more than 11,000 people on the borough's housing waiting list, more than the council's housing stock of 9,000 homes.

And according to the co-operative, Kensington and Chelsea also has the highest proportion of single person households in London.

OPENING the Portobello Housing Co-op's first house were Mike O'Dwyer, Derek White, Gareth Bere, Steve Ross, Raule Harding, Nicholas Paget-Brown and Geoffrey Murray.

KENSINGTON NEWS + POST 2nd July 1987.

5. Portobello Opens the Door (02.07.1987)

The Co-op had now been in existence for seven years and had taken some important decisions on its day to day running. It had decided on various sub-committees answerable to the General Meeting, regarding matters relating to development and short life. It had decided that all members had to be registered on the Council waiting list to prove their housing need and that those only seeking short life accommodation would not be admitted to membership. Initial policies had been passed, such as on rent arrears; maintenance; membership and allocations. It had even declared that anyone wanting to have a co-op wide house-party would have to obtain GM approval!

In the spring of 1986, the co-op conducted a survey of members, with a very high response rate. Although there were two families and two single parents (with a total of seven children) the vast majority of members were single and without children. Less than 20% were unemployed, but of those earning, 70% had incomes of less than £100 pw with 20% receiving less than £40 pw. None of the members had come from a secure tenancy and all were in housing need; almost half had been renting from private landlords, the other half from being in temporary accommodation or living with friends. The survey found 60% had been in K&C for more than three years before joining and ten members had remained members since the beginning in 1978/79.

Harassment Continues

In the earlier part of the 1980s there had been clear indications that some landlords in the area had been obtaining vacant possession against tenants in order to sell on (sometimes even to housing associations) at inflated prices. By the middle of the decade this had not slowed. The Chief Executive of Kensington and Chelsea Council reported to its Health and Housing Committee, on the 23rd September 1985, with figures for the amount of annual, reported illegal evictions at 60 and reported new cases of harassment, at 350. He stated "....... the majority of complaints derived from areas where there is a high concentration of houses in multiple occupation, such as Earls Court, South Kensington and Ladbroke Grove. The reason for this is well established, namely the desire of landlords to convert properties from bedsitting room establishments to houses containing larger flats. In order to reap financial benefits of such conversions, landlords require vacant possession of their properties with consequent conflicts over security of tenure and the provision of alternative accommodation." In the same year, the Courts recognised the emergence of "sham" agreements from landlords seeking to circumvent the protection given to tenants by the law. The case of *Street –v- Mountford* [1985] found that Courts must look behind what's on the face of the agreement, for the real intention of the parties and the real factual position. If the occupier actually had security, they could not be evicted without a court order.

However, events in the rental sector of fundamental importance were occurring in W11. At the end of 1984 and early 1985, five large fully tenanted properties in and around Holland Park, had been bought by one of the most notorious landlords in the history of renting. Nicholas van Hoogstraten had a past. In 1968 he was jailed for arranging a grenade attack on the home of a Rabbi and demanding money with menaces. Later, he was jailed for breaking into premises; evicting elder tenants and conspiracy to damage property. Other sentences, for bribery and receiving stolen jewellery, followed.

Almost immediately after the houses were bought, tenants began to receive threats to their personal safety, with oral and written abuse from Mr. van Hoogstraten, who described them as "scum". The utilities in a number of premises were restricted and in one house, in mid-winter, the elderly caretaker was told that if he touched the hot water, he "would have his hands cut off". Tenants sought urgent assistance from a rights centre, through whom a group of women occupiers led the formation of a tenants association and the Council was lobbied. After much persuasion, eventually, robust decisions were taken at the highest level with the Chief Environmental Health Officer, Graham Pike allocating a number of tenancy relations officers to take details of the allegations and in October 1985, all five properties were taken into public control on the basis of the "health, safety and welfare of the occupants". This was a draconian power and could be followed by the issue of a Compulsory Purchase Order (C.P.O.) under which the properties would be bought, taking them away from the individual's ownership completely. These CPOs were made shortly afterwards.

NEWS TIMEOUT 28/01 1987

HIGH COURT BACKS TENANTS

A Department of Environment inspector who refused to hear evidence of alleged harassment against tenants of rogue landlord Nicholas van Hoogstraten (above) has had his decision overturned by a High Court judge.

The inspector, presiding over a public inquiry into whether Kensington and Chelsea Council were correct to compulsorily purchase five of Hoogstraten's properties, had insisted that the law only allowed him to judge the matter on the basis of the bricks and mortar condition of the properties.

But the council, prompted by Hoogstraten's campaigning tenants, argued that long-standing harassment was at the core of their decision to confiscate the properties and that the relevant evidence had to be considered by the inquiry.

The result of the judicial review will be welcomed by a host of London boroughs who, for 20 years, have been unable to proceed against rogue landlords because of the DoE's narrow interpretation of the law. A rash of Compulsory Purchase Orders on the grounds of harassment are now expected to follow, but a solicitor acting for the tenants this week warned the councils to exercise care. 'The High Court ruling,' says Mike O'Dwyer of North Kensington Law Centre, 'does not indicate how serious harassment has to be before councils take action. It would be unfortunate to say the least if councils jump in rashly and take draconian action only to be overturned by a court of appeal. This would take us back to where we were before this week's ruling and will shut the door on important cases in the future.'

The DoE could, in fact, log an immediate appeal against last week's decision as could counsel acting for Hoogstraten. This would further delay the public inuiry and cause more strain for the embattled tenants. However, a spokeswoman for the tenants pledged this week that they would carry the battle to the end.

Andrew Tyler

Oct 25 1985 KENSINGTON NEWS

Town Hall siezes five houses 'for safety of residents'

FEARS for the safety of people living in five houses in Kensington controlled by one landlord have led to a dramatic move by the Town Hall, *writes Peter Mulligan.*

All five houses have been taken over and put into the safe keeping of the Council.

Locks were changed immediately after the control orders were made last Wednesday.

Confiscated

The move means the houses, worth millions of pounds, are confiscated from the landlord for a period of five years.

Sources say the action is "unprecedented," because the main

dens and Holland Park.

Notices were served at up to 12 addresses because the landlord is said to operate under many aliases and to be a mysterious figure.

The house at Norland Square was handed back to the landlord last year after being the subject of a previous control order.

The Council hired a private security firm to watch over the houe, as the *News and Post* reported last year.

"We have a lot of evidence that those particular houes are not only badly managed, so that they are in a bad condition, but also of harassment to the tenants.

"The action we have taken is for the health, safety and welfare of residents," said Housing chairman Richard Walker Arnott.

Notices

The notices were served on Image Property Ltd. of Old

6. Action Against Rogue Landlord (1987)

Mr. Van Hoogstraten immediately appealed. It was clear that the financial stakes were high and the Secretary of State ordered a public Inquiry. All parties instructed legal teams, the tenants turned to the Law Centre Housing Unit, who organised representation and also acted for other local advice agencies making submissions. Almost immediately the proceedings were halted with the Inspector ruling that only matters relating to "bricks and mortar" were relevant (thus excluding allegations of mistreatment to tenants). Proceedings were started in the High Court to challenge the ruling and after a lengthy hearing in January 1987, Mr. Justice Taylor quashed the Inspector's ruling, stating that if by reason of a landlord's conduct, a tenant was being harassed or intimidated, it was a "callous use of language" to say they were provided with proper housing accommodation.

After further lengthy delays (during which the tenants remained protected due to the control orders made in1985) the resumed public inquiry was set for December 1987. Shortly before it was due to resume, Mr. van Hoogstraten withdrew his objections and within a few months the CPOs were confirmed. In 1988 the five houses were sold to local housing associations, subject to the rights of the existing tenants. Mr. van Hoogstraten was jailed in 2002 for having a business associate killed.

The Co-op Celebrates

Having secured its first property and created its first three permanent tenancies, the members of the Co-op thought it was time to take stock. It decided to have a reception in the new house at 79,Tavistock Road W11, to thank everyone who had helped. It didn't stop at that. It wanted to have the Co-op ethos recognised and celebrated more widely – so it produced a glossy publication, "*Portobello Housing Co-operative – the*

First Eight Years", launched at the reception in June 1987. In it, the Co-op described itself as"small but sound" with the following characteristics:

"We are a fully mutual housing association, registered with the Housing Corporation to occupy permanent accommodation in the North Kensington area of the Royal Borough of Kensington and Chelsea. All members of the Co-op have an equal say in its running. We aim at the acquisition, development and management of property, without profit, for the purpose of providing public, fair-rented accommodation."

The document went on to set out a brief history of the Co-op's development since 1978; to launch the results of the1986 members' survey as referred to earlier; to describe the basic policies and structure; also, the importance of short life housing and the experience of buying/converting the first house. The document went on to make an impassioned plea for more co-operative housing, whether long or short term, management or permanent, as an additional form of housing tenure.

Here are some concluding remarks:

"We are firm believers in sharing experience and so rather dry tasks are switched around from time to time with a back-up of assistants learning what to do and taking over. We are far from perfect and if everything ran smoothly we would be the first to be surprised."

"...we are extremely pleased to see that in its Strategy Statement for the next five years, the (Housing) Corporation has resolved to attempt, in conjunction with the Borough, to develop a forward strategy to meet the housing need of those involved in small Co-ops. Of course finances are strictly limited, but this Strategy is to be applauded as giving some hope to those of us who have battled against the odds, for years."

The event attracted good press interest, "*Housing Associations Weekly*" (03.07.87) celebrated the opening of the house, showing Co-op members gathering outside and noting that, "Kensington and Chelsea is a Borough where 44% of households are single persons, and it has a severe housing shortage. There is a waiting list of 11,000 people whereas the council's stock amounts to only 9,000 properties". Again, the "*Kensington News and Post*" (02.07.87) showed dignitaries at the reception, including the Director of K.H.T., Geoffrey Murray and the (then) new Chair of the Council Health and Housing Committee, Nicholas Paget Brown. The article mentioned that PHC were the first Co-op to receive funding from the Council and put the cost of the first property at £150,000.

Also celebrating, of sorts, was a member who had joined the Co-op the year before. John Mead was single, homeless and had been living in a squat in Dulwich when a couple of friends who had contact with the Co-op suggested he join the Council housing waiting list and apply. He explains,: "I was very lucky, I moved in to short life within days of joining but it had very little "life" and we had to move out quickly. After moving again, I spent some time in a place in Blenheim Crescent W11. That was very different short life, some people had been there for quite a long time and there was a mixture of Co-ops in a number of houses. It was a bit like a colony."

Now that 79 Tavistock had been completed, a new Development Officer was needed and John Mead was appointed to the job. He explains his role, "Our development agent was K.H.T. and I worked with their Development Department (Richard Clark and his assistant Rosemary Sandham) to prepare the annual bids for financial allocation from the Council. This involved projecting how much an acquisition would cost and adding appropriate amounts for the refurbishment – the total would come to over one million pounds! I and others from the Co-op would also search locally for suitable properties to begin the buying process".

1988 and All That

The beginning of the year saw the publication of a Parliamentary Housing Bill, by the government, which would introduce radical changes in rented housing sector and which would continue to have an effect on the housing market some thirty years later. All sectors would be affected, for instance housing associations would be forced to raise finance on the open market and Council tenants would be given the right to vote for an outsider to take over the running of their estates, However, it was the private rented sector which was to bear the brunt of the changes based on de-regulation of tenancies. Among these changes were:

- "Protected Tenancies" would be abolished for all new lettings;
- New, "Assured Tenancies" would be at full "market" rents and have less safeguards against landlord abuse;
- New, "Shorthold Tenancies" would be the norm and give occupiers no security at all;
- Any rights of succession on death would be hugely curtailed;
- All tenants of resident landlords would no longer have any rights against summary eviction.

Housing law practitioners, Law Centre workers and tenants' rights organisations all began concerted arguments over the Bill. Kensington and Chelsea recognised the implications of this new legislation. In May1988, a report to the Health and Housing Committee stated "indeed it is possible that the Government's plans to de-regulate new tenancies in the sector could lead to an increase in homelessness as more landlords take eviction proceedings against tenants". We shall see later that, 30 years on, the contents of that report turned out to be entirely accurate.

Dramatic events in the spring of 1988 brought these events to the streets of North Kensington after the death of Sir Brandon Rhys-Williams, the M.P. for the area. Sir Brandon, a Conservative Party member, had a good track record on housing issues. He was very supportive on many of the campaigns set out previously and indeed supported the brief passage of the Houses in Multiple Occupation Bill in 1992/3. However, this was different. A parliamentary bye election brings with it an awful lot of national news interest and visiting politicians. The number of candidates was in excess of 15, including the "Payne and Pleasure Party" and "Ladbroke Grove Class War". With the Labour Party candidate, Ann Holmes, being a housing rights activist it's not surprising that housing was an issue. In fact housing was the issue and more surprisingly, private rented housing - the only time recorded that this issue was to be in the forefront of such electoral discourse. The Co-op got involved by co-sponsoring a special hustings on the subject of rented housing, where the implications of the loss of tenants' rights was hotly debated On the 14th of July 1988, the result was that the Conservative majority had been cut from almost 4,500 to 815, with another 4,000 votes against the Government sponsored candidate through other parties. It was a clear democratic message that the rented housing changes were not wanted in Kensington.

Prior to the introduction of what became the Housing Act 1988, some minor changes were won to soften the blow in relation to shorthold tenancies (a six month moratorium from the tenancy start date preventing eviction) and after a rigorous, well argued case to preserve harassment and eviction law, a new civil law remedy was introduced with the protection from eviction criminal offences made easier to prove. The main changes were enacted and remain the basic structure of privately rented tenancies, today.

North Kensington Law Centre had been in operation since 1970 and was about to experience its "Coming of Age". From an original 3, by the mid-eighties, it had 20 staff and from a budget of £9,000 it was now over £200,000. It was still in the old butcher's shop in Golborne Road W10 and it was there that the Lord Chancellor, Lord MacKay of Clashfern travelled to in May 1987, for an official visit. He met clients, staff and management committee and even had time for a quick stroll down the Road, to the corner of Portobello. It was a recognition of the fact that Law Centres had consolidated (from the first, there were now 58) and that the work being carried out was really needed. The *New Statesman* (06.02.87) summarised the approach as follows;

"What really sets law centre staff apart from their high street colleagues and makes them more controversial, is that they have a radical approach to the law. Instead of being content to take each case as it comes, they want to tackle the underlying social causes and eradicate the problems."

7. Law for All - Peter Kandler, founder of North Kensington Law Centre (06.02.1987, New Statesman)

An example of this approach came in 1988, when the Law Centre Housing Unit contributed to a report on what it and colleagues in the Law Centres Network had found, over many years of defending tenants in rental possession cases in county courts:

- Many people don't understand what's going on and don't know how to defend themselves;
- Very few tenants facing rental possession have representation and eviction orders are issued at the rate of one every minute;
- Judges are ignorant of welfare benefit rights; "rubber-stamp" what landlords want and show alarming attitudes to minorities;
- Court buildings, wigs and gowns intimidate and alienate ordinary people.

The End of the Eighties

By 1989, in Kensington and Chelsea, there were still 18,000 households renting from private landlords. Nationally, as regards bedsit tenants, 81% of properties remained unsafe. There had been a second Houses in Multiple Occupation Bill introduced into Parliament in 1987 which again failed despite the fact over 600 people had lost their lives in fire in multi-occupied lettings since the Clanricarde fire in1981 and that 3000 local properties remained uninspected by the Council. Significantly, a 1988 RBK&C Housing Needs Survey carried out by RBKC confirmed that over 40 per cent of those still living in multi-occupied property were migrant workers (see *Behind the Façade*, 1989)

Back in1984, 13 migrant workers who had survived the 1981 fire, had instructed PHC member Mike O'Dwyer at the Law Centre, to bring an action against their ex-landlord. The case was listed for hearing towards the end of 1989 but in September 1989 the landlord's legal team agreed a payout to settle the action. The clients agreed to share a total of £35,000, the landlord's own legal costs bill approaching some

£23,000. Although not a direct legal precedent, the landlord's insurance company clearly didn't think it was worth the chance of having a final trial. Many of the survivors decided to return home (where the money would last much longer) whilst in the U.K. the legal fight continued for proper fire protection for the most vulnerable.

In November 1989, Portobello Housing Co-op received the results of its first full monitoring visit by the Housing Corporation. It covered committee accountability / management control / finance / maintenance / allocations and development. This was a crucial document because if the result was negative, it would almost certainly mean the loss of all finance from the Council. Overall the score was good with some improvements to be made in the detail of membership and allocations. Not surprisingly, participation and accountability were described as "outstanding." Just before this, the Co-op had adopted a procedure for acquiring houses with sitting tenants and due to demand, had imposed a limit of 6 to numbers on its waiting list.

Someone who was particularly anxious whilst waiting for the outcome was John Meade, who had been appointed as the Co-op's Development Officer the previous year. He was present at the main meeting with the monitoring officer "I came back from work to a meeting at one of the new flats at 79, Tavistock Rd. All the officers of the Co-op were there and everyone was speaking. It was probably the first time the monitoring officer had ever met anyone outside an office". John explains that after much searching, a property just two doors from 79 had been found in Tavistock Road, that the development finance had been allocated and it had been purchased in mid 1988. Again, it had been short life'd initially whilst the process of tendering and details of refurbishment continued. John explains "I had to supervise all the paperwork, the development agent would report to me and I would report back to the Co-op.

In the early days I didn't know what people were talking about - it all sounded a bit serious, but organically I became part of it". The property was finished in the spring of 1990 and John received his reward in that he was allocated to one of the units. 75 Tavistock Road W11 was a three storey terraced house and would have been suitable or three single units but there were three members who wanted to share accommodation so the upper floors were converted to that specification. This meant that four Co-op members were housed, rather than three.

By the end of the decade, PHC was looking towards the next development, which it had resolved should be much bigger than any of the two already within its portfolio.

PART 2

DEVELOPMENT AND CONSOLIDATION – 1990 TO 2005

Acquisition of Large Houses

68 St. Marks

By the late 1980's, the Co-op was being allocated by the Council, an annual sum for the acquisition and development of property approaching £1 million. In late 1988, this was largely taken up by the purchase (with development) of a large, mid-Victorian, double fronted, detached property in St. Marks Road, W10. It was unconverted, run-down and had several sitting tenants of a private landlord. P.H.C. was persuaded to go ahead with the purchase following an agreement with Kensington Housing Trust (KHT) whereby they would re-house the tenants in exchange for nominations to its membership. The Co-op changed its rules to provide for new (ex-sitting-tenant) members and a development agreement was signed with the Trust. This Development Agreement provided that KHT would act as agents of PHC on the technical aspects of the conversion – each of the individual developments were covered by similar agreements. In exchange for 3.5% of the project price, KHT would manage the tasks, for example, all supervision of work on site; plans and specifications; the payment process; practical completion and associated processes. However, the Co-op would remain responsible for obtaining funding; final approval of plans; tenders and completion.

Plans were drawn and a specification of works drawn up to provide 6 single flats with one family unit (conversion cost £220,317). The process of re-housing sitting tenants began, the Co-op appointed one member exclusively to liaise between the tenants and the Trust; and to ensure that offers of accommodation appropriate to needs were made. As units became vacant, the Co-op drew up short-life licences so that members could occupy units as temporary accommodation. In parallel, the Co-op was entertaining nominations from the Trust with a view to the new members being housed in the property. Unfortunately none of those nominated felt that the Co-op was an appropriate home for them, having regard to the necessary commitments associated with membership. Eventually, it was agreed that none of the sitting tenants would be re-housed back into the property and that accommodation would be provided by KHT.

The works were completed at the beginning of 1991 and the 9 members allocated moved in. From the family unit allocated, member, Sharon Landau recalls that she, her partner and very young daughter had been in 5 separate properties in the five years before settling into St. Marks. One person doesn't forget the experience of 1990-91 - it meant he could show his commitment to the Co-op and finally settle down. Simon Morrissey was a young man who had been squatting in London during the '80s but who knew someone who was an early member of the Co-op. In 1989 he was persuaded to go along to a meeting and apply for membership. Whilst going through the lengthy process of attending meetings, in spring 1990, it became clear that the Co-op needed its own "development officer" to oversee the conversion of 68, St. Marks Road. Although merely a "prospective-member", Simon stepped up to the plate and agreed to help out, subject to reporting-back to the G.M. After his membership came through, he was rewarded with a permanent allocation to 75,Tavistock Road, W11 because someone had moved out and into St. Marks. Simon went on to spend 4 years as Secretary to the Co-op and today is its Chairperson. He comments on his housing: "*As a single person in the '80s, I had no chance of being re-housed. I was desperate for an official permission to occupy – it was the first I ever had*" and he recalls, "*you were never allowed a telephone whilst you were squatting – after my allocation, I had a 'phone – I could 'phone my mum.*".

196 Ladbroke Grove

From 1989, the Council restricted its funding to special needs so the Co-op turned to the Housing Corporation for funding. The bid in 1989 was unsuccessful but it was thought another should be formulated. A new member, Maureen Pepper, agreed to take the task on, she had helped out on development whilst waiting for membership. Expertise was called on and detailed arguments formulated showing how housing need would be met through proposed projects. Following a presentation by Co-op members, at the London office, funding approaching £1 million was granted for purchase and development, subject to a full inspection by a senior regional officer. The Co-op welcomed this, not only because it wished to be accountable for the expenditure of public money, but also because it represented a comprehensive evaluation of its working methods. The review involved consideration of General Meeting minutes; various policies and procedures (both implemented and planned); financial records; development experience; members' skills and workload. The findings were released at the beginning of 1991 and included recommendations for more financial training; keeping rent arrears low and more investigation into maintenance of stock. The officer commented "a notably stable and cohesive group with high levels of participation....skills and workloads are spread across the members." Various pending policies also needed to be implemented (see later).

This was enough to release the funds. With unbounded enthusiasm, Maureen had proposed she be made development officer for the next property and had set about searching the streets for appropriate potential properties, in anticipation of the outcome. By the time of the funds release, a property had been identified at 196, Ladbroke Grove Wl0. This was typical of many multi occupied houses in the area at that time. It had been allowed to decline into an appalling condition, for 10 bedsits there was one water tap in the stairwell and one outside toilet. Living conditions were disgusting. It also highlighted a common lack of intervention by the local authority to protect residents. In anticipation of the sale, the landlord had "got rid of" the tenants, despite the best efforts of the Co-op to intervene.

Shortly afterwards, in March 1991, a Development Agreement was signed with KHT and the works went on site in early spring. The conversion was to include a large maisonette, with three other single units. The allocations process took place in mid 1991 and for the first time there was in-built participation by prospective tenants in the eventual design and lay-out of the units, fulfilling the Co-op's aim of tenants having control over their own housing. Maureen Pepper spent almost full time being the Co-op' development officer until completion of the project, in October 1991. She was rewarded with an allocation to one of the finished units in November of that year. The family allocated to the maisonette had a tale to tell. Sandy Scowen had come to the U.K. in 1986, from her home in New Zealand, to work on an Antipodean publication helping new arrivals. On a low income, with one young child and pregnant she was compelled to move into a property in Latimer Road, W10, which she thought had been completely abandoned and condemned. One day in spring 1988 she received a visit from a delegation – it turned out to be members of P.H.C., she was squatting in a Co-op short-life property! It was clear that Sandy had improved the conditions in the property no-end and rather than return it to the Trust, the Co-op decided to let the family stay, on condition that she immediately apply for membership of the Co-op. Sandy finally became a member in December 1988 and was moved into two short-life properties before being allocated to 196, Ladbroke Grove, in 1991. Still there now, she comments "the Co-op has always been there for me. For the majority of my life I have brought up my family in a Co-op house. My children have now moved away but they love coming back".

Policies and Procedures

The Co-op had established basic operating rules (such as membership and allocations) from its inception; however, they were far from comprehensive and had not had the benefit of practical experience. In contrast, a code for the occupation of short-life property had been developed and implemented since the mid '80's. With the coming of the "permanent properties" it was necessary to have procedures which reflected both good practice and the ideological spirit of the Co-op.

Membership

The comprehensive membership policy was approved in June 1990 and slightly amended late in 1991. There were to be three criteria for the selection of applicants:

- Housing Need (had to show lack of, or unsuitability of, occupied accommodation along with having joined the Council's housing waiting list)

- Connection to the Borough (by fact, work or family)
- Commitment to the Co-op (by showing a series of attendances at General Meetings and engagement with tasks whilst waiting to join)

In addition, a full procedure for dealing with applications for membership was established, using the above criteria. In November 1996 the procedure was amended by adding a membership group which would look after the prospective member through the process. Over the years the number of membership vacancies has varied but one thing has remained constant since May 1979 – the total maximum of 30 members. A decision was taken at the outset not to expand beyond 30 in order to provide for a sense of community and for better peer-relations. The decision to run Co-op business through General Meetings, open to all members rather than through a management committee, reflected a desire to keep the Co-op both inclusive and democratic. The membership ceiling was thought to provide for this.

Tenancy

As the permanent properties came on stream, there was a need for a standard tenancy agreement which set out the contractual rights of landlord and tenant. The Housing Act 1985 had excluded tenants of "fully mutual housing co-operatives" from any type of security of tenure; nor were they to have the same rights as council or housing association tenants. These tenancies were to be "contractual" and (subject to limited external rights) the only protection coming from what was agreed in the tenancy document. In addition, the terms had to be within the rules of the Co-op as it could not grant anything it did not have power to under its constitution.

In January 1991, the Co-op drafted and approved its tenancy agreement. It is still in use today in its original form. Some guiding principles reflected the politics of the Co-op. Tenant-members were not to profit from occupation (i.e. no equity was to be taken out when a member wanted to leave) and there would be no right to buy (or any other method of disposal). Highlights included:

- The agreement was dependent on the tenant remaining a Co-op member;
- Possession proceedings would only be taken under defined circumstances and after due process;
- Full lawful repairing obligations would apply to both parties;
- Significant restrictions on sub-letting, taking lodgers and succession.

As a general rule, the Co-op had decided that any changes to the agreement would affect all tenants equally. Perhaps the most important agreement was for the payment of rent. As the permanent properties were new conversions, the rents had to be set afresh. To do this, in 1991 -2, the Co-op approved a method of rent setting. Standard features in the flat were "pointed" that is, given numbers for features such as dwelling type / numbers sharing common parts / heating installations / gardens and external / plus any extras. The full points score in total was divided into the Co-op's total annual operating costs to reach a "multiplier". That multiplier was applied to the individual points score for each flat, arriving at the total payable. The principle behind this method was that the cost to the tenant should be no more than the cost needed by the Co-op to provide that housing (without profit) and to run the Co-op's business generally on a prudent and financially viable basis. The same principle applies today.

Allocations

The Housing Corporation's review at the beginning of 1991 had highlighted gaps in the Co-op's method, particularly in the context of moving into property ownership. Although fair treatment was at the heart of the Co-op's ideology, it had not been written down and therefore it could not be seen to be being followed. Therefore in the autumn of 1991, a policy was framed which recognised the need for fair and equal treatment of both members and prospective/potential members, without any discrimination. The policy resolved that the Co-op would treat all applicants equally and ensure as wide a catchment base as possible. This would extend to all contractors engaged on work for the Co-op. Matters would be monitored.

At the same time the Co-op was documenting the process whereby a member would be allocated a tenancy. As this was its greatest gift, the process was critical. The detail would be carried out by a sub-committee of the General Meeting to which it would report with a final recommendation. Deliberations would be based on the following

- Basic equal treatment of housing needs for all applicants;
- Applicant compliance with Co-op rules and history of attendance at meetings;
- Rent arrears history;
- Experience of and commitment to the Co-op.

Any appeals process would go through the General Meeting, initially.

Repairs and Maintenance

The final part of the jigsaw as regards the establishment of a code for the occupation of permanent housing was to provide for a fair and reasonable process for dealing with repairs and maintenance. It had been recognised in the standard tenancy agreement, that both the Co-op as landlord and the member as tenant, had obligations concerning the upkeep of the property occupied. Central to the process was the Repairs Officer, to whom disrepair was to be notified (by definition, ongoing maintenance was less important at the outset but was to become dominant later as the stock grew older). The Officer was to keep a record of all repair jobs. Repairs were classified into varying degrees of response times. Emergency repairs were to be carried out immediately; followed by urgent and then routine matters. Tenants had remedies if responses were inappropriate. In addition, the Co-op was to carry out annual inspections of areas retained, along with gas safety checks and 5 yearly decorations of the common parts.

The Repairs Officer would arrange for jobs to be carried out, with various numbers of estimates being sought from contractors (the more costly the job, the more estimates were needed). The General Meeting would approve the contractor and the start of works. The Officer was then to supervise the repair work and on completion, with General Meeting approval, would instruct the Treasurer to issue payment. However, any work carried out by a Co-op member (whether the tenant or otherwise) could not be paid, in accordance with the rule introduced by the Housing Associations Act 1985 which prevented a member of a "fully mutual housing co-operative" from receiving any financial remuneration. The repairs process was to change with time as the volume increased to reflect the age of conversions, but the general principles still apply.

The Wider Picture

Throughout the 1980's, North Kensington had seen a serious decline in the volume of accommodation available to let as privately rented units. Before that, it had been the dominant sector, with the amount of social housing provided by the Council historically low. We have seen that the Council had been persuaded to invest in funding housing associations which, throughout the decade had expanded, buying much of the stock which had hitherto been let out by private landlords. However, the discounts introduced by government to incentivise those wishing to take advantage of the right to buy scheme had increased, and were taken up - with the result that the volume of public sector properties available for letting decreased (1,500 Council properties being sold in Kensington by 1994).

8. Kensington Park Road W11 Mixed media on paper, 30cmx40cm, (2016) Justin Earl, see cover details

These trends continued through the 1990's, including various schemes to allow housing association tenants to require their landlords to buy for them (this was not particularly successful in North Kensington due to property prices). The rise of the housing association movement continued through the decade; indeed some would say that RBK&C operated its own housing stock through them. By the end of the decade, Notting Hill Housing Trust owned 2,000 properties in the area. Although a very desirable area to acquire social housing, sales were kept relatively low due to the contrast between council and housing association tenants' rights to buy. Analysts have pointed out that the "multiplicity of tenure" in North Kensington owes much to the retention of HA stock at this time. However, the association stock was becoming increasingly dilapidated. For instance, the first purchases of Notting Hill Housing Trust had been converted way before the 1974 Housing Act funding regime was introduced. These were (550 properties) mainly in the Colville area of North Kensington and needed almost £13 million spent on them (by 1995) to bring them up to an adequate standard. Disrepair would continue to be a common problem and would reflect corners cut following reductions in funding for property conversions, in the first place. The associations also found themselves constrained by the Council requiring, "nomination rights" to developments funded by Council money. These rights could mean that up to 75% of new units in a development would be prioritised for those coming through the Council system, leaving very few units for the Associations having developed them . The vast majority of these nominations were, "homeless persons" to whom the Council had a duty laid down by law – it was in fact the way in which the Council overwhelmingly complied with its responsibilities, without having the "burden" of the tenants. Also, demographic changes meant that many more groups without accommodation were presenting throughout the decade. Examples included those with refugee status and people suffering from AIDS and other related illnesses such as HIV+). Meanwhile, single people were still trying to cling on to their ties with North Kensington.

In mid-1993, the Notting Hill Council of Churches published a report on housing need in North Kensington, as a result of increasing deprivation. It found that despite the Borough having the highest house prices in the country, the North was both overcrowded and within the top ten most deprived areas nationally. Over 100 languages were spoken and the area was still a crucial abode for those in the service industries. There were at least 4,000 people on the Council waiting list, many of them single, living with friends and having no hope to be re-housed. Rough sleepers had begun to appear with at least fifty people habitually sleeping out. Government initiatives such as the "City Challenge Partnership" (an input of new funds from Government, designed to stimulate commerce) were at best cosmetic (this proved to be true); there needed to be urgent, combined, community and statutory action. The churches recognised that a house is "*...much more than simply a roof over one's head, it's the place where a person creates and lives out life...*" P.H.C. was listening. The report concluded by proposing the building of a "*minimum of 50,000 new affordable homes in London*". This was written over 25 years ago but applies equally today!

Many of the members of the Co-op had previously been squatting vacant property in order to find accommodation in central London as a result of the shortage of affordable accommodation. By the mid-'90's, squatting was still active as a result of the continued housing shortage, particularly for single people. In response, the Government drafted the Criminal Justice and Public Order Act 1994; it was the first step towards the criminalisation of squatting. The Act took away the protection that previous legislation had given to someone, who whilst occupying property, opposed the entry, by force, of someone else. Two sorts of people now had a right to use force to enter. First, a "displaced residential occupier" (someone who had occupied immediately before the present entry) and secondly, a "protected intended occupier" (specifically for council dwellings) who had been allocated the property, immediately before the present entry. A failure to leave was a criminal offence and the occupier could be arrested. It was not to be the end of the battle over squatting.

Faced with increasing numbers of homeless persons and with severe shortages of accommodation in which to house them, the government decided to restrict the eligibility of applicants to homeless services, by amending homelessness legislation and introducing immigration control into homelessness law for the first time. In 1993, a law removed the right of asylum seekers to any type of temporary or permanent accommodation if the individual had access to any accommodation, regardless of its nature or condition. Shared hostels were provided for the completely destitute. For someone who had been forced to flee their country and was applying for refugee protection, this amounted to degrading treatment.

However, the attempts to restrict legal rights for the homeless did not stop there. A series of decisions by the higher courts declared that anyone accepted for re-housing by the local authority could not insist on either any basic standard of accommodation or for the housing provision to last for a minimum amount of time. Eventually, the Conservative government, which had been in power since 1979, cut back homelessness rights to the bone. The Homelessness Act 1996 enacted:

- That the duty to house any homeless persons to whom a duty was owed, was limited to two years;
- Any housing could only be provided through the rules as set out in local allocations schemes;
- A new internal local authority review process was introduced, to re-examine decisions made and keep them out of the courts (the '202 review');

- No homeless accommodation whatsoever could be granted to asylum seekers;
- European Union nationals became subject to immigration control, the onus being on them to prove that they were exercising treaty rights.

In terms of council tenancies, the age-old concept of security of tenure was swept away by the Act which brought in, "introductory tenancies". These tenancies meant that within a fixed period of a year, any new tenant would be liable to eviction without any pre-designed reason and there was no way of challenging this in a county court. Kensington & Chelsea Council adopted the new concept immediately.

Also in 1996, the council made the most fundamental change to its role as a housing authority. It decided to give up its role in managing its housing stock and on the 1st April 1996 it entered into an agreement with a new Company, *Kensington & Chelsea Tenant's Management Organisation (TMO)*, to carry out the day to day jobs involved in being a landlord. These included lettings/collection of rent/possession proceedings/local repairs and tenant management issues. The Company was designed to break even; would have nominees from the council, co-opted experts and some tenants on the management committee. Almost 10,000 units were transferred to the TMO; about 20% of that number had already been sold off under the Right to buy legislation. The council retained overall ownership of the stock (and responsibility for housing the homeless) but in 2002, the role of the Company was extended to cover, "major capital works" which included improvements, modernisation and programmed repairs (this gained access to extra Government resources). It is within this function that it undertook external cladding to the structure of Grenfell Tower which was to lead to the horrific tragedy in 2017 (see later).

9. Grenfell Tower 1 (August 2017) Michael O'Dwyer

The following year, in May 1997, there was a change in the national administration, after nearly two decades, with the Labour Party winning the general election by a landslide. In housing terms, the first relevant piece of legislation was not immediately obvious, probably because it was so groundbreaking, but it became increasingly significant as the years went on. The Human Rights Act 1998 incorporated into English law, the provisions of the European Convention for the Protection of Human Rights (1950). Several provisions are outside the scope of this study, but the three most relevant are:

- Article 6 – the right to a fair hearing;;
- Article 8 – the right to respect for home, private and family life;
- Article 14 – the prohibition of discrimination in exercising those rights.

There were various barriers built into the legislation to prevent easy use of the rights as a shield to existing legislation or precedent and although laws could be declared incompatible with the Convention, they were then not automatically repealed. There was an extended period of delay before implementation of the legislation on the 2nd October 2000. Immediately, housing lawyers began testing the scope through the Courts. Assured short hold tenancy automatic possession; summary eviction of introductory tenants and elements of disrepair law, were all found not to be incompatible with the Convention, whereas mainstream possession actions were found to engage Article 8 (without changing much). There was a flurry of legal action in the first three years of coming into force. This was followed by notable gains including succession rights for same sex partners; an increasing awareness of human rights in homelessness cases (despite a reluctance to overturn findings of fact) and the reconstruction of the appeals system in housing benefits disputes.

On the squatting front, the noose was tightened even further by the introduction of the 2001 Civil Procedure Rules (a Code for how the Courts operate) which introduced a fast track process for regaining possession. A legally rightful ex-occupier (within rules) could obtain an "interim possession order" in a civil court which would enable them to enter the premises at will. Any unlawful occupier refusing to leave after the granting of an interim order was committing a criminal offence and could be arrested. As is so often the case with this type of legislation, the very threat of the use of this procedure would end squatted property and the homeless would again be "moved on".

At first, homelessness legislation was left intact by the Labour administration but by 2002 the calls for reform had grown too loud to be ignored. The Homelessness Act 2002 finally overturned the restrictions in the amount of time homeless persons could be housed. It also extended the definition of homelessness and cleared up some of the other anomalies built up over the years. It strengthened the review rights of applicants in the light of bad decisions by local authorities but it left alone the immigration provisions so severely criticised.

In terms of law reform in rented housing, the statutory Law Commission held extensive consultations between 2002 and 2005, to "adopt a consumer approach to regulate the landlord-occupier relationship". The two social housing provider networks, that is, local authorities and housing associations, had different codes when it came to security of tenure and tenant's rights. Equally, the regime for privately renting had been in operation since the end of the '80's with varying degrees of satisfaction. The main recommendations were:

- Standard written tenancy agreements for both the public and private sectors, the terms of which would bind all parties;
- Standard terms to apply and only exceptionally to be varied;
- All possession actions to be started by appropriate and prescribed notice documents;
- Automatic possession to remain for private lettings with Court discretion in the public sector.

Some of the proposals were thought to be controversial but the consensus was that the attempt at modernisation was timely. The Commission eventually produced a draft Parliamentary Bill but it was not taken up (by successive Governments) and the law of rented homes remained a hopeless maze of legislation and case-law. Regrettably, the proposals remain "on the shelf" to the present day (although the Government has recently indicated it may be interested in "streamlining" rented accommodation legislation in some way).

The second major piece of housing legislation actually enacted in this period was the Housing Act 2004. Its main provisions had to do with housing conditions in rented dwellings. The established standard for dwellings to be "fit for human habitation" (last enacted in 1985) was replaced by a new system of rating for, "hazards". Enforcement provisions by local authorities remained largely the same and were re-enacted. This was to become controversial many years later with the Grenfell Tower fire in 2017, when many housing lawyers blamed the lack of enforceable rights by residents, as having an effect on events.

Part 2 of the 2004 Act set up the first formal and dedicated procedure for regulating the management of houses in multiple-occupation (HMOs). A comprehensive statutory definition was introduced and it was made compulsory for the larger properties to be licensed by the local authority. Councils could also introduce licensing schemes for smaller properties after consultation. Licenses would be granted on condition of good management practice which would include the status of the landlord. Adequate conditions of occupation would be a prerequisite for approval. Letting without a license was a criminal offence. It was now over twenty years since the tragedies of the early 1980's in this type of vulnerable letting (see Part 1) but this reform was welcome nonetheless.

Also in the 2004 Act, the Government agreed to set up a system whereby the deposits of renters would be protected within schemes, during the currency of the tenancy. There had been an outcry at the amount of money (amounting to millions of pounds annually) being lost (by those who could least afford it) to landlords who unlawfully withheld deposits at the end of tenancies. In the legislation, if the deposit was not properly protected, the landlord could not use the fast track possession route and cold be liable for up to three times the deposit in damages. These were universally acclaimed as progressive.

Meanwhile, the volume of Council tenancies continued to contract, with the numbers of those presenting as homeless increasing. By 2005, the numbers of sales under the right-to-buy had passed 1.5 million nationally.

Housekeeping (1)

The later 1990's saw the Co-op dealing with the realities of home ownership and the practicalities of collectively managing members, some of whom had now been in the Co-op for 20 years. The most fundamental rule was that all members must attend the General Meeting which was the supreme decision making entity, with apologies only being allowed in defined circumstances. This was considered necessary because the GM was (and is) the body through which all the work is defined and all the important decisions are made and transacted. A rule was instituted that any prolonged absence would have to be approved and that in any event an absence of more than 3 months would automatically terminate membership. As the continuation of tenancies (and short-life licences) was dependant on continued membership this could have severe consequences.

By the spring of 1997, the Co-op's finances were becoming complicated. There was a mixture of permanent and short-life rents coming in; repair and maintenance outgoings; fees to pay to housing associations (for short life licences) in addition to ongoing running costs. A set of financial procedures was passed to both safeguard matters and to provide a recognised method by which financial transactions took place. The structure was divided into three parts:

- Practicalities of payment. Access to the books; cheque signatories, approved persons etc;
- A petty cash system, access and accountability;
- Authorisation of proper expenditure through the General Meeting structure; material needed to support and policy framework for significant amounts.

Finance was such an important part of the life of the Co-op that it was a standard item on the General Meeting agenda. Particular methods were also introduced to deal with repeated expenditure (such as the repayment of the mortgages on the owned properties and for the protective investment of excess funds).

It would be irresponsible not to recognise that amongst a body of people living closely together, there would from time to time be conflicts of varying degrees of severity. Most conflicts were resolved early and informally, but some progressed, or were of a nature which touched all members. By mid 1997, the Co-op recognised that it needed to have a policy for dealing with formal complaints. Again, the GM was to be the arbiter but it was recognised that the presentation of potentially sensitive subject matter; the need to assist some parties and the "due process" of investigating and determining disputes, necessitated the establishment of a "Complaints Officer" from within the membership. This was not a job that most would welcome doing but it was backed up (as with all officer roles) by a job description setting out the role. The Officer was to interview the parties, collect relevant documentation and attempt mediation but if that didn't work, to present a fair report to the GM for decision. The Officer was further available to assist parties with any appeal, which in the first instance would go to a further GM and thence to the Independent Housing Ombudsman which had its own Complaints Procedure. The Co-op joined the Ombudsman's scheme in March 1997; its orientation was to consider whether the policies and procedures of the organisation had been exercised with fair and reasonable execution.

Further Acquisitions

With the ownership of four properties, from 1992 there was consolidation within the Co-op and less of an emphasis on the search for new acquisitions. Public finances had dried up, leaving the open market as the only source of purchasing and development. In addition, during the decade, house prices had increased substantially in North Kensington which had started to become a "desirable" place to live. Historically, the Co-op had been looking for whole houses, with ultimate vacant possession and in need of conversion, which would be costed at such a rate that the repayment burden would not be excessive in the context of affordable rents. Any large properties were being swept up by very rich purchasers to the extent that there were no potential properties available. A debate ensued between those who believed the Co-op should be more flexible in its search for new accommodation and those who wanted to hold out for another large, local acquisition.

By 1996, a development committee had been formed. There were still members in short-life accommodation; some had been there for a considerable time and wanted to join those in permanent properties. The Co-op had indicated that anyone who was a prospective tenant should be part of the committee. Quite separately from this, the Co-op decided to carry out an exercise to see what it needed to put aside for major repairs to its permanent properties. It instructed a firm of surveyor's to inspect for probable defects and armed with that, in 1997, it instructed a housing financial consultant, Bob Williams, who turned probable defects into amounts to be deposited into a separate fund to abide the events. Mr. Williams also analysed the finances of the Co-op having regard to that provision. The result was that the Co-op had, unrestricted funds of over £100,000. This changed the debate about the nature of potential new property, the Co-op recognised it could spend money and still be financially viable. It also decided that the property search could extend into the adjoining areas such as Shepherd's Bush, Harlesden and Willesden. Maureen Pepper, who was part of the Committee, remembers that "we spent long afternoons in offices trying to explain to estate agents what the Co-op was..." Eventually someone saw particulars for a one bed property in Kensal Rise, part of a mixed use building and not in need of conversion. After GM agreement, solicitors were instructed and the property was conveyed (on a 99 year lease) in January 1998. The person allocated was Jim McIntyre who had joined the Co-op in 1994 and who had just been forced out of Co-op short life as the housing association wanted the property back. Shortly after moving in, Jim became the Secretary of the Co-op, a post he still holds today as the Co-op's longest serving single office holder. As a postscript, a year later, another, very similar property in the same building came onto the market and with the obvious advantage of "clustering", the decision was taken to purchase the further one bed-roomed unit, again on a 99 year lease, with completion in September 1999.

Housekeeping (2)

By 1998 the exercise of the Co-op's finances had become extremely complicated for the voluntary membership, still meeting every alternate Friday for 2 hours. In April 1998 it was decided to contract out the bookkeeping and financial oversight, to a secondary housing co-operative (that is a housing co-operative made up of other housing co-operatives)

Co-operative Housing Services. They took control of the rent analysis and a report to the GM; production of rent accounts for individual tenants; recording of income & expenditure and liaison with the auditors for the annual exercise. Recommendations to the GM were made in relation to the updating of financial procedures in accordance with Co-op decisions.

The accepted norm for the level of rent arrears in social lettings is 4% of the total rent roll. Very rarely has the Co-op gone over that figure and most times the arrears figure is well below. However, there have been individuals who have left matters go to such a level that the ultimate sanction of possession proceedings has been contemplated. The Co-op has had a rent arrears policy from the first day it started to occupy short-life stock, in the early 1980s. This policy provided for the production of rent accounts so that the occupier could see what has been paid and what is due. All payments due and made by all occupiers were (and still are) presented to each GM, where anyone in the meeting can challenge a payment record. It was called "peer pressure" and has succeeded in keeping arrears low. If arrears were more than a few weeks, a notice to quit would be issued and the property handed back to the housing association. This action had to be ruthless because the Co-op was paying a licence fee to the association and it would be losing money from day one. As regards the permanent properties, the Co-op at first used the short-life template but it became clear that something more sophisticated was needed. Therefore, in March 2003, after many months of drafting and discussion, a new Rent Arrears Policy was adopted. There were a number of clear steps that everyone was subject to:

- Anyone over 6 weeks was to receive a warning letter;
- Over 8 weeks, a second letter requiring a repayment plan and attendance at the next GM;

- Over 8 weeks and in breach of repayment plan, GM decides service of a notice to quit;
- Last chance to re-pay but if not, Extraordinary General Meeting decides on the commencement of Court action.

Each individual step would be examined at the GM; the policy was designed to give the tenant all opportunities to meet their responsibilities and explain to the GM before ultimate action was taken.

10. General Meetings

In the early years of the millennium, the Co-op had a fundamental look at its complexion and how the members felt about the organisation. There had been a fall off in attendance at General Meetings which had lead to inquorate meetings (see below) and a lack of people available to fill the tasks needed. A survey was carried out, based on the following questions:

- How have you contributed to the Co-op?
- What skills and qualifications do you bring?
- How can you contribute? What prevents you?
- Your hopes and fears for the future?
- What have you gained from the Co-op?
- How to affirm commitment?

The response rate was almost 70% and a group was formed to analyse the results. In the responses, hopes were expressed by members that long term absenteeism would be replaced by active involvement; that planning for the future and taking stock were important and that development into a community with ecologically sustainable practice, were goals. Fears were expressed that the Co-op would fold; that re-engagement would be difficult without a lack of clear direction and cohesion. Overall, responses were firmly for the continued provision of permanent housing in an accountable way and for a modest expansion of membership. A vigorous debate ensued which threw up two major proposals. The first was the establishment of a "management committee" structure to run the Co-op. Eventually this was rejected because the establishment of a small group would end the right for all members to have an equal say in the decisions which governed their lives and was "giving in" to the non participation of others. The second proposal was to reduce the quorum figure for GMs downwards from 8 members. This figure had been established in 1979 and is incorporated in the Rules. It is quite a high figure bearing in mind the actual membership at any time can be as low as 26. The significance is that if the quorum is not reached, no business can be transacted other than that for information. No decisions which bind the Co-op can be taken and it paralyses the Co-op from action. All matters would have to be put over to the next meeting and if that itself was inquorate, the Co-op would be unable to operate. Again, this was seen to be the thin edge of the wedge and avoiding the problem of non-attendance by making it easier for the Co-op to operate. Instead, the Co-op undertook intensive action with those not attending and the problem was solved without structural changes.

"25 Years – Let's Celebrate"

2004 was the 25th year in the life of the Co-op and in January the GM decided to organise a series of celebrations to mark its silver jubilee. A budget was set at £5,000 and delegated authority passed for transactions. A planning group began to meet, at first monthly then bi-weekly in the run up to the weekend of the 24th of July 2004. Tasks were broken into three sections; the search for ex-members; preparations and running the major-event party.

The search for ex-members was both intense and time consuming. A list of 130 was produced from shareholding records and each member of the planning group took a list. It was agreed to produce an exclusively designed, commemorative T-Shirt (gold on cornflower-blue with a "Portobello" crescent on the front, "25" and "1979" on the back). 300 were produced, two for each current member (only to be collected at meetings) and one for each invitee, with the rest being sold at the Party at almost cost price. It was clear that everything would hinge around the Party on the Saturday night. Permission was granted from an ex-member who had produced the artwork for the cover of the 1987 publication, for the image of North Kensington and the Westway to be used for a poster and for the invitation. In addition to members past and present, invitations went to local community groups and to significant individuals from the Co-op's journey. In response, written tributes and best wishes were received from senor officials at both the Council and the Housing Corporation.

It was agreed that, as a counterpoint to the main event, there would be a quieter and more relaxed time for members to reflect and celebrate the moment. It was agreed that this would be a barge trip on the Regent's Canal. An application for a contribution towards the funding was made to the North Kensington Amenity Trust and a grant of £300 was forthcoming. On the 10th July 2004, thirteen Co-op members embarked "The Beauchamp" at Little Venice, Maida Vale for a slow cruise up to Camden Lock whilst the sun went down on a sultry summer's evening. Complete with captain and bar, everyone brought food, music and memories of the Co-op's journey so far.

You Are Invited To

the 25th Birthday celebration of

PORTOBELLO HOUSING C0-OP

On Saturday 24th of July 2004

At " Parrish's " Club, St. Charles Sq. W10

(see map)

- 8pm till late
- Full catering
- 3 live bands
- Legendary compere
- Sound system
- Late bar.......

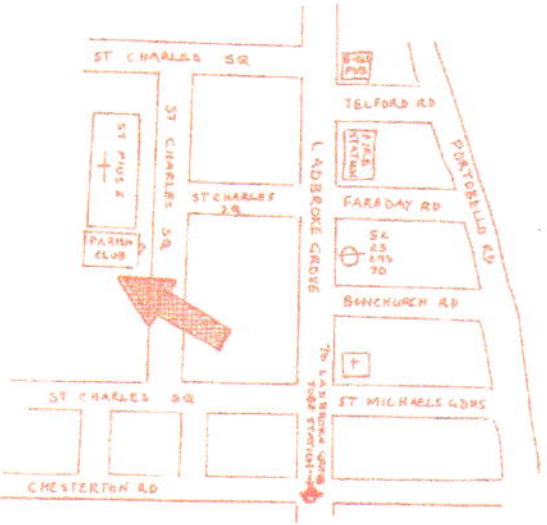

And On Sunday 25th of July (weather permitting)

A " Picnic in the Park "in St. Mark's Park, St. Mark's Rd W10 (opp No. 68) from 1pm.

(bring supplies)

RSVP: 79, Tavistock Road, W11 1AR

11. Invite to the 25th Birthday Celebrations (2004)

As for the Party, a local community club ("Parish's") in St. Charles Square W10 was hired and a late license obtained. Someone made a banner which read, "PHC – 25 – So Far". Full catering was arranged ("Ethel Minogue Associates", Celtic-Fusion) and it was agreed to engage a Texan filmmaker, Robert "Bucky" Hartnet, to record the whole event. As people arrived, interviews were recorded. Here are some extracts:

Gareth Bere (who for many years was the Co-op's treasurer and one of the first permanent tenants) "I joined in 1982 after 10 years squatting. The Co-op is a step towards housing for single people. I was happy to be housed because I love the area".

Phil Winstanley "I joined in 1981, my first memory of a Co-op meeting was under the Westway in a meeting-room called, the Pit. After the meeting we all went round the corner to the Elgin Pub on Ladbroke Grove, where there was a reggae sound system. My experience with the Co-op helped me get a job with a housing association and as a result, I made it my career."

Payley O'Connor and Raul Harding "We were friends, squatting in Sirdar Road W11. I knew this guy, Dave Lightfooot and he was a member of the Co-op. He asked us if we wanted to take control over our housing and we took him up – that was 1982. We were offered short life in Barlby Road W10 almost immediately but it was uninhabitable – no plumbing nor heating, the windows didn't even have glass. We spent all our savings doing it up, we did all the work ourselves – we had learnt the skills squatting." (Raul) "I stayed there for well over four years until the first permanent house came up and I was allocated a one bed flat in it. I am still there. Although the Co-op has had some rough times we have kept our vision – to house people and keep the organisation going. We're proud and it feels like family, it's like a community".

Tessa Mcthreddar "I was squatting in Sirdar Road W11 in 1984 when someone told me about the Co-op and I went to meetings. I became a member and in 1985 I was allocated short life in a house in Blenheim Crescent W11. There were a number of other Co-ops occupying short life along the same street and it was like a little colony, with us all interacting and hanging out together. In fact, that's where I met my husband Alan and where we got married. Sometime later we decided to move to Brighton but I must say that PHC was vital to us, it gave us a sense of stability and allowed us to build our family together".

Nicole Denny "I have been a member for 15 years. I found out about the Co-op from the Housing Corporation, they gave me a list. I wrote to all of them but Portobello was the only one to reply. The homelessness re-housing system discriminated against single people. After joining, I was in two sets of short life during which time I became the development finance officer for the newly acquired property in Ladbroke Grove. I was very grateful to get the chance to work. I was lucky to be allocated to one of the permanent units in due course."

The line up for the Party evening was as follows:

Compere	–	Tony Allen
M/C	–	Simon Pinder
8.15 To 9pm	–	Acoustic Set from Steve (W.11 Housing Co-op)
9pm to 9.15	–	Comedy set from Tony Allen
9.15 to 9.30	–	Formal Addresses from Mike O'Dwyer

9.30 to 10pm	–	Alan & Dave (Country Blues)
10 to 11.30	–	Dave Nolan and The Healer Band (solid Rock n' Roll)
11.30 Onwards	–	Dave Brown's Sound System

Mike O'Dwyer summarised the Co-op's history and reminded everyone of the founding intentions – provision for single people in the area, a determination to succeed out of self help and to retain control over the provision and management of housing. Thanking the planning group and those working on the night, everyone raised a glass to the next 25 years!

During the evening, "Bucky" the filmmaker continued to interview members and ex-members and here are some more extracts from the transcript:

Sean Canning (who at the time was the Director of North Kensington Law Centre, still operating in the Golborne Road W10) "I joined the Co-op in 1998, with my partner Rachel. We could not afford to rent in the private sector and as single people we had no priority for re housing. It was like walking into a family, with a mixture of more senior members and others finding their way. We moved in to short life in 1999 and the next year we had our fist child. Unfortunately young James' health was not good and he really needed access to a garden. After a couple of years we scraped together a deposit and bought a place - with a good garden – in Kensal Rise but I have to say that the Co-op gave our family a start, a vital time to stabilise our household."

Tom Vague is a local historian and music expert "PHC has thrived through Thatcherism but we're more like communists, we're neither Socialists nor Tories. We have succeeded in keeping ordinary people in North Kensington as well as the rich. If you do empower people, it can work."

Maureen Pepper (who spent the whole of the '90's in the Co-op) "Above all, being in the Co-op was FUN. There were great people, the meetings were rather jolly, if not a little tedious at times – and there were great parties. I had great conversations with people about poetry; bands; Berlin; art; travel; avant-garde; theatre and so on".

Finally, a couple of the newer arrivals:

Helen Thorpe "I joined in 1999. I was living in the area and had set up a community business. I needed to be close to the business for service reasons but couldn't afford rental values so I was staying with a friend. Unfortunately there was no short life around when I needed it so I had to spend an extended time out of the area. Eventually I moved in to Co-op short life. I have taken responsibility for recording the minutes of the General Meeting and distributing them to members. It's a vital job."

Piers Butler (painter and artist) "Guitar Bob told me about the Co-op and I joined about six years ago. I was lucky to get into short life quickly and I responded by volunteering for the post of short life officer – that is chasing new short life and looking after what we've got. I've also done the role of membership secretary, keeping records of who attends General Meetings and answering queries from people who want to join. The Co-op is a remarkable bunch of people managing to run our own housing and control our own destiny."

PART 3

2006 TO 2018 – THE MODERN ERA

Co-op Developments

Conflict and Resolution

The Co-op had developed a complaints system in the late '90s (see earlier). Although rarely used, it was to be tested to the extreme between 2007-2009 and ultimately found wanting.

The Co-op's largest property had gardens both to the front and back, yet the tenancy agreements were silent with regard to how they were to be used and managed. Arrangements had developed ad hoc over the years, with those tenants interested using areas to plant and grow bushes, shrubs, flowers, herbs etc. From 2004, two tenants fell out with each other in respect of the management of some of the plants. Matters deteriorated, including verbal abuse, physical conflict and interference with plants. From time to time either party would bring aspects of the conflict to the General Meeting without any overall resolution. This included an agreement (in 2005) to draft a "use of garden protocol" but this was not acted upon at the time.

Eventually, in June 2007 one party brought a formal complaint against the other alleging both nuisance and harassment. The complaints procedure took until December 2007 to report to the General Meeting which was not satisfied with the methods used and rejected its findings. The Co-op then found itself unable to progress matters when proposed outside arbitration was rejected. Finally, in summer 2008, one party referred the matter to the Housing Ombudsman's Service. Interim garden management measures were implemented pending the outcome.

In May 2009 the Ombudsman found that the Co-op's complaints procedure was inadequate with regard to matters such as nuisance, harassment or anti-social behaviour. Therefore the Co-op had no means by which it could effectively investigate and resolve disputes covering these matters. This was compounded by a lack of clarity in the role and remit of the General Meeting within the complaints process. There was a need to improve procedures; to revisit the existing complaints procedure and to swiftly reach decisions on the existing complaints. On receipt of the Ombudsman's findings, the Co-op engaged an independent expert from a company specialising in Housing Co-operative systems, to urgently advise on proper management systems. After reviewing all of the documentation, it concluded, in June 2009 that:

- There was an urgent need for a garden use protocol delineating identifiable areas between tenants;
- Need for a clear statement setting out definitions of each nuisance, harassment and anti social behaviour, with proper approaches to complaints in each category;
- Both parties had been less than courteous to each other; had not shown reasonable respect to each other and had engaged in unacceptable conduct.

Very shortly later, the Co-op called an extraordinary general meeting to consider both reports. It issued apologies for the delay in resolution, together with appropriate warnings having regard to individual behaviour. Very shortly thereafter, it finalised its protocol for the use of gardens throughout the Co-op and it revised the complaints procedure to be clearer on gathering witness statements. The procedure was also amended to include a comprehensive section on harassment. Finally, in June 2011, the complaints procedure was further significantly amended to include a complete section on issues of anti social behaviour and clarification of the role and remit of the General Meeting in decisions. Meanwhile use of the garden at 68, St. Marks, had become academic as the front and most of the rear gardens had been decimated in preparation for the major works at the start of 2010 (see Appendix 1).

The condition of the stock

By 2006, most of the permanent homes owned by the Co-op had been occupied for between 10 and 15 years. These properties needed upkeep and one of the tools for doing this was "cyclical maintenance". This was (and still is) a process whereby the structure and fabric of the building would be rendered "wind and watertight" to prevent deterioration over time. The works were set to take place on a five yearly cycle, in rotation, with one (or sometimes two) buildings each year. When its time came up, each property would be surveyed and a specification of works drawn up. A member of the Co-op (possibly from the house) would be appointed to co-ordinate matters for the duration of the project. Common elements of work would include: refilling masonry and pointing brickwork; painting external woodwork; overhauling gutters, gullies, roofs and drainage. The common parts would also be redecorated. The specification would be put out to tender (to at least three contractors) and the results would be considered by the General Meeting, with the job being let on the Co-op's standard contract. The Co-op's representative would liaise with the contractors and the residents, throughout, making regular reports on progress to the General Meeting.

The average cost of works in 2006 was £8,000 but would obviously vary depending on the size of the building and inflation.

There are legal obligations in respect of repairs, on both the Co-op as landlord and the tenant as occupier of a unit of accommodation (mostly set out in the standard tenancy agreement). Most importantly, the Co-op is responsible for the structure and exterior (and the delivery of services) whereas the tenant has to act in a reasonable manner as occupier. In 2010, the then repairs officer brought together both the legal elements and established Co-op practice in a "*Repairs and Maintenance Handbook*" which was distributed to all members. The preface read:

> "Portobello Housing Co-operative is committed to
> Ensuring that you have a real opportunity to
> Influence decisions which affect your home.
> Get involved – make a difference!"

After setting out the respective responsibilities of landlord and tenant, various items of potential disrepair were listed, in tabular form, with boxes showing where the responsibility lay. The Co-op policy for activating remedial work, was set out – emergency items, 48 hours, urgent items, 7 days and non urgent, as soon as possible. The handbook ended with a section on tenants' alterations and what to do if dissatisfied. It was distributed to all members and became known as, "The Green Book", by the colour of its cover.

Also in 2010, discussions over a policy to compensate tenants for the distress and disturbance associated with major works were finalised in the context of the subsistence underpinning at the St. Mark's property (but also forthcoming replacements/ improvements). The Co-op recognised that, for whatever reason, a need for major works would cause serious disruption to the tenant in two ways; clearly within the flat itself but also within the immediate surrounding area including the common parts. As regards the interior, the sum awarded would be equivalent to 20% of the rent, times rooms affected, times length of disruption. As regards the surroundings, the Co-op would settle on a lump sum to reflect length of time affected and level of interference. All this would be in addition to out-of-pocket expenses. It was applied to the tenants in St. Marks Road and paid in February 2011 (see Appendix 1).

By 2012, most of the properties had been occupied for between 20 and 25 years. Many of the fixtures and fittings, particularly in kitchens and bathrooms were coming to the end of their natural life and would soon need replacing. As long ago as 1997, the Co-op had recognised the need for future planning and conducted an exercise for replacement over a 30 year period. During the winter and spring of 2011/12, a group of members were asked by the Co-op to consider the subject of replacements of bathrooms and kitchens within the whole of its properties. In June 2012, the report proposed that there should be a rolling programme of replacements, starting with the earliest conversions (unless the occupier wished to defer action). It further proposed that a "refit brief" be drawn up with the occupying tenant ("maximising value and minimising disruption") and proposed to the GM for approval. At 2012 prices, the cost for the whole Co-op was estimated to be £110,000, this to be paid for by a one-off rent increase of 10% across the board. The amount of the increase was to be ring-fenced exclusively for the replacements with any excess being applied directly to their individual property. Not all members were comfortable with the proposal and the matter was shelved. The issue remains outstanding today.

In March 2013, the Co-op revised its procedure for dealing with repairs. The procedure hitherto had been diverse, with some tenants carrying out their own repairs (using skills gained from their time spent squatting and living in short life) others going through the repairs officer and some suffering the disrepair silently. The new procedure provided for a "Maintenance Officer" (MO) who would convene a "Maintenance Committee" made up of one representative from each of the Co-op's houses. Any tenant with defects would contact the house representative who would inspect and bring the matter to the Maintenance Committee without delay and the pre-existing division into emergency/urgent and non urgent jobs, would continue. The Maintenance Officer (MO) would bring a report to each General meeting including new matters for decision as well as update on existing jobs. The MO would take exclusive responsibility for dealing with contractor, including obtaining tenders, signing contracts and payment. Later in 2013, the Committee carried out a survey of all tenants to get a picture of the amount of work to be done. The returns identified a number of day to day matters along with themes such as inadequate windows; and of heating systems and defective flooring. This maintenance system continues today, although it is fair to say that as the stock ages the issues become both more frequent and complicated resulting in the need for more resources.

An important aspect of property upkeep is safety, the most important of which has been the annual landlord gas safety check. This has been a statutory responsibility on those who let property, since 1998 and it is designed to ensure that the gas supply to rented premises is in proper working order (including the primary appliances for the use of that supply). So seriously does the Co-op take its responsibilities in this matter that it has, on one occasion, had to issue legal proceedings against a tenant to obtain an injunction to require access. The Co-op engages a specialist firm of gas engineers to check on the safety of all appliances and requires access to each flat during a concentrated period in October every year. This firm (Professional Gas Heating Services (PGHS) also carries out the servicing of the central heating systems in all the Co-op's flats and is by far its longest serving contractor. Peter Batkins, a founding director of PGHS comments:

"We have had the pleasure of carrying out all aspects of gas safety and heating repairs for the Co-op, in all their properties. What's been enjoyable about serving the Co-op has been building relationships with everyone – as it's been pretty much all the same people over the years. The Co-op is one of four long standing clients of ours and we hope that it continues for years to come."

On the subject of household safety, in 2015 the Co-op required all tenants to install smoke alarms in their flats (supplied by the Co-op) and this was extended to carbon monoxide alarms in 2016. More recently still, in the context of the Grenfell Tower disaster (see later) the Co-op has embarked on a fundamental review of all fire precautions in all the properties.

What's the Co-op worth?

Rule 4 of the Co-op's governing instrument states: "The Association shall not trade for profit" therefore it is not the aim of its activities to make money. Of course it is subject to the same regulations as similar organisations in that it cannot continue "trading" unless it remains financially viable. By virtue of an Act of Parliament in 2014, the government created a recognised structure for Co-ops, to be regulated (now) by the Homes & Communities Agency (and see later the discussion on regulation generally).

The Co-op has always had its accounts audited on an annual basis. Recent changes have meant the need for a formal "audit" has been waived for small societies but in actual fact the same depth of investigation is done by the same firms now known as "independent accountants". Ever since it began occupying property, the Co-op has engaged arms-length assistance with the practicalities of internal finance administration. Today it engages a consultant to keep written up the books of account and rent records; to report on financial developments to the General Meeting and to oversee the annual financial checks by the independent accountants. Every year, the books and supporting materials are sent away for analysis, returning some months later with the draft "Annual Accounts". The procedure is then governed by the Co-operative and Community Benefit Societies Act 2014; an Annual General Meeting is called at which the draft Annual Accounts are presented for consideration and approval of all members.

The information in the accounts is pretty standard each year and is designed to give the reader an honest picture of the state of the Co-op's finances. The main notice points for any reader will be the overall balance of the assets; changes in turnover (rent roll) and running costs; provision for major repairs; the cost of maintenance; the yearly surplus (deficit) and the amount available to add to reserves. After the annual accounts are approved, they are sent to the regulators for lodgement as part of the Annual Return. At the same meeting, all the officers and deputies of the Co-op are elected for the coming year.

The Co-op is lucky enough not to have ever had a deficit and to continually be able to have added to its resources. This is mostly due to the fact that for over 30 years the yearly activity has been constant: the provision of residential accommodation for its members. As a general picture of the Co-op's financial position over the past decade, the following are the average figures for some key elements in the annual accounts, for the decade since 2006:

- Yearly routine maintenance expenditure - £10,200
- Holding in major repairs reserve - £162,000
- Holding in cyclical repairs reserve - £22,000
- Yearly rent from permanent properties - £62,800
- Yearly running costs - £24,120
- Yearly surplus - £22,763

From time to time the Co-op has had strategic meetings with its independent accountants to examine wider questions than annual expenditure. Matters covered have included:

- Present rent levels and future expenditure plans, particularly the replacement of original infrastructure;
- The practicalities of dealing with provision of property for an ageing membership;
- Prudence and the extent of resources;
- The question of re-mortgaging existing properties to raise finance in order to expand housing provision.

In 2006 the Co-op carried out a "value for money" exercise in order to consider whether it was using its resources effectively. Its research found that there was a high level of participation by members with all the various jobs filled and an average attendance at General Meetings of over 60% of the membership. With no employees, all the general work was carried out by the members, allowing rents to remain low, after allowing for costs of repair and reserves. Accordingly, in contrast with other public housing, members were not as reliant on work-related benefits and further, the use of low cost, local builders with minimal overheads kept the cost of day-to-day repairs down, allowing reserves to be built up.

Insurance

The Co-op is a multi-property owner and in accordance with its responsibilities both to its members and the public in general, it must be covered by insurance for its activities. There are two types it maintains, primarily in relation to the properties it owns (although its two leasehold interests are dealt with by the freeholder) and also to cover the administration of letting those properties. In order to cover the various elements of these two areas, the Co-op engages the services of an expert broker which specialises in the field of not-for-profit housing providers. The annual process is that the Co-op's insurance officer (i.e. one of the members) will make an annual return, confirming the nature of the stock together with any changes from the previous year and any matters which may give rise to a claim (known or ought to have been known). Apart from the matters set out in Appendix 1, the Co-op has only had one other claim in its entire 40 year life. Upon receipt of the return, the broker obtains quotes for the various elements of requirements and outside new claims any increases should only reflect market changes. A formal quote is produced by the broker and if approved by the Co-op's insurance officer, is put to a General Meeting for ultimate decision. The elements of the insurance portfolio are as follows:

- <u>Property stock</u> – This covers all permanent properties (save leasehold) and is aimed at re-instating damage to buildings and associated areas (including fire, flood and subsidence);

- <u>Combined liability</u> – Aimed at business activities, particularly to cover liabilities to third parties due to Co-op action;

- <u>Commercial crime</u> – Losses due to fraudulent activity, to include internal theft;

- <u>Legal expenses</u> – Protection against external commercial legal action.

The Co-op has spent approximately £6,000 annually on its insurance obligations. For the Property stock policy, the permanent properties have to be valued for their "rebuilding cost", that is to reinstate the fabric of the building so that, after decoration, it may be let again. In 2012 the properties were re-valued and since then have been increased at industry rates so that today the value stands at some

£2,700,000 (much less of course than any valuation for sale on the open market).

The local picture

All Saints Road

Since the middle of the twentieth century there has been a large Afro-Caribbean community in North Kensington. This group experienced extreme racism shortly after arriving in the 1950s (see the Preface, above) responding by forming self-help community groups and establishing Carnival as a political statement. It remained over represented in social housing and the privately rented sector, due to poverty. During the 1970s and 1980s its youth were the subject of heavy handed policing which lead to much resentment. Over the years, second and third generations have emerged but the whole community was stunned when, within 18 months, two of the most respected leaders passed away.

In 2008, Gladstone Robinson, from Jamaica (known as "Sledge") died after living in North Kensington for over 50 years. He was one of the first waves of West Indian immigrants to arrive in the U.K. Sledge Robinson was reputedly one of the first to wear dreadlocks and in his later years his flowing white strands made him uniquely recognisable. He was a committed Rastafarian and was instrumental in opening the first local Ethiopian Orthodox church, in the late '70s. He was also a prolific musician who played with many of the leading reggae bands throughout his life. He was caught up in police tactics of mass arrests for suspected cannabis use, being seriously assaulted in one bogus raid in the mid 1980s. He finally received some compensation and remained widely respected until his death.

Frank Critchlow passed away in 2010. He came over from Trinidad in the 1950's, settling in North Kensington and in the '60s he had a cafe (the "Rio") which was in and out of the news at the time, due to political scandals (e.g. the "Profumo Affair", mentioned in the Preface, above). During this time he built his reputation as a civil rights campaigner; he was also outspoken in defence of the rights of black people; in favour of the legalisation of cannabis (though against the use of hard drugs) and an advocate for protection from police harassment. It was not surprising then that after opening a new Caribbean restaurant ("*The Mangrove*") at 6-8 All Saints Road in 1968, it was raided 12 times in the first 18 months. Eventually a community protest march was organised but broken up brutally by the police. Frank and others were arrested on multiple charges but finally, two years later, a jury acquitted everyone charged with incitement and resisting arrest. So began two decades of conflict between police and the Mangrove. During the 1970s, the area around the restaurant became known as "the front line", where the consumption of cannabis developed into a political act and its use so prevalent that dealers would use All Saints Road as an office. The area became a popular place to "hang out", attracting media stars, musicians and the bohemian sub-culture. The Mangrove became a space where community activity was planned as well as being a Carnival organisational base occasionally. The Mangrove Steel Band was born and went on to be a core element in Carnival, practising each year, immediately outside the restaurant for weeks in the run up to the Carnival opening day.

Finally the authorities decided to change the nature of the Road. In 1982, the Apollo Pub closed down. This had been a distinctly multi-cultural place with no frills and a reputation for very loud reggae sound systems, but the owners decided that it was "selling more grass than beer". It was rapidly acquired by Notting Hill Housing Trust, who by this time had diversified into running commercial ventures. The Pub was converted into a number of units for workspace and an area devoted to a recording studio (which eventually, in the 1990s, became the base for the girl-band, "All Saints", who went on to international stardom). In the decade that followed there was a concerted attempt to improve the appearance of the Road, described by one pundit as a "£1 Million police designer makeover". Gentrification had arrived.

In 1988 the Mangrove restaurant was raided on a number of occasions with Frank Critchlow again arrested in a violent manner, this time charged with supply of cannabis and heroin. This resulted in a serious riot at the close of Carnival and it was clear that the community was very angry at police enforcement activity. Some 18 months later, Frank was again acquitted of all charges, but the bail condition that banned him from the premises meant that the restaurant finally closed. The fact that he was later paid a considerable sum of damages by the police for false imprisonment, battery and malicious prosecution couldn't prevent the banner which read: "The Mangrove - 21 Years of Resistance" being finally taken down in 1991. The Mangrove Community Association opened almost immediately, in premises directly across the Road from the restaurant and for a while the area continued with its "front line" status, particularly at Carnival, with the Steel Band and a number of the leading sound systems using the Road as a venue. By the end of the 1990s, shop rents had significantly increased and residential property prices had soared leading to a demographic shift and the return to what might be described as "an ordinary road".

Legal Aid

In the new millennium, North Kensington Law Centre was still functioning from the old butcher's shop in Golborne Road. Now over 40 years old with continuous delivery of free legal advice and assistance to those in need, an ex Portobello Housing

Co-op member, Sean Canning, was appointed Director in 2003 and was to steer the organisation over the next 10 years. He reports an increasingly difficult environment for the less well off in the area, particularly those reliant on benefits; those subject to immigration controls and anyone looking for a solution to insufficient or inadequate housing. The Right to buy had continued to diminish Council stock, with no replacement units being provided for those lost (and the resultant contraction in the volume of social housing available). In the private rented sector, landlords were able to charge higher rents for properties; and complaints of disrepair were met with the threat of eviction through lack of security. National legislative changes added to this restrictive environment and the result was an increase in Law Centre housing casework, mainly caused by both increased homelessness and tenants falling into rent arrears.

The Law Centre itself had grown to employ 16 staff by 2003; its funding came from a combination of legal aid revenue, small charitable giving and an underwriting grant from the central Lord Chancellor's Department. The time was right for it to be restructured to make it more business-like, which in turn attracted new finance from the local Council (an increase from £1k to £60K in five years). The mix of work reflected the pressure points of poverty in the area but some new areas emerged, such as advocacy for excluded school pupils and legal rights for vulnerable adults subject to trafficking. One area of work which the Law Centre had pioneered at the beginning was the representation of tenants at county court possession days where litigants on their own were offered help to stop an eviction. Along with colleagues from North West London Law Centres, lawyers and paralegals participated on rota – for many years without payment – and prevented thousands of evictions. It continues today, finally and belatedly recognised by the mainstream legal aid system.

2007 saw major legal aid cuts in the civil law system, including housing work. The restrictions hit all types of practitioners, from independent legal advice centres (including Citizens Advice Bureaux) to lawyers in private practice. It was a two pronged attack, firstly, in order to be paid for work, "suppliers" had to contract with the Legal Aid Board and secondly, both the amount of work and the rates of payment were restricted. The result locally was that the Law Centre's revenue reduced considerably. Many legal aid firms were forced to close or merge, including for example, Sinclair Taylor & Martin, in Thorpe Close W10, the only general private practice in the area which, after more than three decades moved out and ultimately closed.

The legal aid cuts were compounded six years later, in 2013, when, following the Legal Aid, Sentencing and Punishment of Offenders Act 2012 (LASPO), the government removed many areas of legal aid from funding. Significant sections of those with legal problems were unable to obtain the help of a lawyer, such as those with personal injury accident claims and welfare benefit claimants trying to obtain entitlements, the latter in the context of increasingly complex rules and regulations. In housing law terms, help with disrepair disputes was severely restricted with tenants required to prove "severe hardship" before being eligible for help and assistance. One of the most pernicious changes was the limitation of any access to legal aid for those experiencing relationship breakdown. In order to qualify for help, an individual had to produce evidence of having suffered domestic violence, with strict time limits, this happening whilst the client is traumatised. Finally, in 2017, following widespread criticism, the government relaxed the rules on family matters and announced a fundamental review of the changes. However, this did not stop the loss of funding in all areas of social welfare law and the resulting contraction in the numbers of lawyers willing to take up legal aid work.

All these changes had negative financial affects on the Law Centre and in recent years it was forced to downsize following staff redundancies. Perhaps the saddest result was that in

2015, it was forced to vacate its premises on Golborne Road in which it had started, some 45 years earlier and to abandon its presence on the street, for offices in a converted car park at the base of a tower block in W10. This move was precipitated by increasing gentrification and higher rents in the Golborne area which made it difficult for the Centre to remain.

Estate Development

This gentrification on Golborne Road had been started in the early years of the century. The largest tower block in West London, "Trellick Tower" was situated at the east end of the Road. It had been notorious in the 70's and 80's for squalid conditions but with many of the original tenants forced to move, the Council invested in a new type of occupier. The largest housing estate in the area of North Kensington was known as the "Murchison Estate", it stretched from behind Golborne Road to the top of Ladbroke Grove housing over 2,500 household in 530 units. When faced with widespread dilapidations in 2006, the landlord, Kensington Housing Trust (KHT) found it could not afford to carry out the work needed on the stock, despite it being less than 25 years old. It decided on an option termed "complete development" which meant abandoning exclusive provision of social housing and becoming a developer with mixed stock of rented and owner occupied units. They foresaw more units within the same area and the project would be part paid for by selling off half the new development. In the process, historical lock-ups for market traders on Golborne Road would be lost; a number of existing tenancies would disappear, as would a section of the only open space in the locality, Athlone Gardens W10.

12. Trellick Tower W10" Isobel Brigham (2001)
oil on canvas 11x10.5 ins

It took until 2010 for the finance to be put together and to obtain planning permission (including demolition). In March 2011, KHT issued a "Residents Charter" containing "Ten Commitments" essentially promising that life for tenants would continue as normal and that there would be full consultation throughout. Any hopes of mutuality were dashed some seven months later when it was announced that the Housing Trust had stopped trading and had merged with another housing provider to become a larger Association, known as "Catalyst Housing", to whom it had passed ownership of the estate. Thus, Kensington Housing Trust, which had been working in North Kensington for almost a century to alleviate poverty and help those in need, disappeared.

K.C.T.M.O.

We have previously seen that in 1996, the local authority, the Royal Borough, had transferred the whole of its rented housing stock to an "arms length" committee of councillors and tenants' representatives, to deal with day to day maintenance and tenancy issues. In 2002 the Kensington & Chelsea Tenants' Management Organisation (KCTMO) took over responsibility for repairs to the stock of almost 10,000 units. The whole of the Council's Housing Department was transferred over (200 personnel) whilst responsibility for homelessness provision remained centrally (see below). Very soon, critics began to challenge the lack of transparency and accountability from governance and management, particularly the lack of a concentrated community base; the presence of a strict hierarchy within officer employees; a lack of transparent representation; extended periods of Board membership and a failure to respond to complaints.

There was particular concern amongst tenants living in high rise blocks, such as Grenfell Tower, a 24 storey building on the Lancaster West Estate, in W.10, with 127 flats. In 2004, an investigation into a failure of emergency lighting in the building found that maintenance had been defective and that the whole system would have failed in an emergency. This was confirmed by an independent report in 2005. Residents were further alarmed, in 2009, when a fire in a similar tower-block, in the London Borough of Southwark, killed six people. Subsequent investigations into that fire found that fire precautions were inadequate, with residents' ill –informed on the means of escape. Again, in 2012, a fire risk assessment at Grenfell Tower found that the sub-contractors responsible had failed to maintain the means of escape equipment in proper working order. Residents' protests failed to result in appropriate action, a result of which was the formation of "The Grenfell Action Group" to represent those living in the tower-block.

As for the residual responsibility for homelessness (left with Kensington & Chelsea Council) increased homeless demand coupled with a shortage of housing stock, made it difficult for anyone seeking assistance. The numbers of those in temporary accommodation to whom the Council had accepted a duty as homeless, increased by a third between 2012 and 2016. This is a clear indicator that there was nowhere for these people to go (because the duty was that the local authority had to provide temporary followed by permanent accommodation). Another indicator of an overall shortage of accommodation was the number of "rough sleepers" (an annual census is carried out of those people actually living out in the open on a given night). These figures more than doubled in the years between 2010 and 2016. Further, in 2017 the Charity SHELTER analysed homelessness pressure points, giving Kensington & Chelsea the 5th highest in England; this despite the Council having some of the largest financial reserves in the U.K.

The Wider Picture

In 2007, a number of financial institutions in the U.S.A. failed due to holding inadequate securities. This reverberated and peaked in September 2008 with the crash of Lehman Bros., a sprawling, global bank having connections with banks, building societies and financial markets in the U.K. There followed a domino effect here, with many of those institutions connected becoming financially unstable themselves. The government intervened with a combination of full and partial acquisition of the most vulnerable, leaving some to fail entirely. The Central Bank also stepped in, introducing historic low interest rates as well as making cash injections into the economy. Meanwhile, consumer retail spending dropped and during the financial year 2008/09, a "recession" was declared. In order to recoup the cost, the government began to limit public expenditure, a practice which became known as "austerity".

There followed many examples of cuts to the revenue of public bodies (such as to local government; the NHS; the Police etc.) but for our purposes, we concentrate on those in receipt of welfare benefits and who are renting. Among these:

- In 2008, the Government introduced a "Local Housing Allowance"; a cap on housing benefit being received by those privately renting, based on a combination of local rent level analysis and a maximum number of rooms deemed appropriate. Many people found that they were forced to leave their settled homes as the revised benefit wouldn't meet the rent. In April 2013 the concept was extended to the public sector with similar consequences;
- In September 2013 an overall benefit limit was introduced (a" benefit cap") whereby adding together a number of eligibilities, a household could not receive more than a prescribed limit of finance. It particularly hit large households hard. In the first three years of implementation, 160,000 possession orders of accommodation were made;
- In 2013, a new benefit, Universal Credit was introduced to amalgamate several entitlements. It has been implemented slowly across the country with extensive criticism of its inflexibility and the hardship caused by waiting times;
- For those with disabilities, life became more traumatic between 2013/15 when Disability Living Allowance was phased out and replaced by the Personal Independence Payment (PIP). Everyone in receipt of benefit had to be re-interviewed and new criteria were applied, particularly as regards matters of mobility. There was widespread criticism of the standards of assessments and the withdrawal of benefits to the most vulnerable.

The inception and continuation of those measures was carried out by the Coalition Government of the Liberal Democrats and Conservatives which took office in 2010. It also enacted two major pieces of housing legislation, both designed to give public sector landlords more power over their tenants and to make life easier when they dealt with the homeless. The Localism Act 2011 introduced "flexible tenancies" whereby Councils could offer fixed-term tenancies (of at least two years) to new tenants. For existing tenancies, after the tenant's death, succession would be limited to the spouse only (previously it could extend to a member of the family). Local councils dealing with the homeless could discharge their duties by offering an Assured Shorthold Tenancy in the private rented sector (thus bypassing long-term security of tenure). Five years later, the Housing & Planning Act 2016 tightened those provisions. The fixed term tenancies (between 2 and 10 years) were now made mandatory, marking the end of the Council Tenancy for life. Any succession granted to new tenants was to be made in a similar manner. Incentives were introduced to encourage housing associations to sell to sitting tenants, at a discount, mirroring the Council's Right to Buy.

However, in an acknowledgement that all was not well in the private rented sector, the Housing & Planning Act 2016 introduced a framework for Councils to establish registers for landlords from which it would be possible to identify those deemed unsuitable and in appropriate cases to apply to a Court for a "Banning Order". That said, it has taken until April 2018 to implement the legislation. As regards multi-occupied lettings in particular (i.e. houses occupied by more than one household) as we have seen much earlier in this document, they can attract the most notorious "rogue landlords", with sometimes tragic consequences. In December 2017, the Housing Minister announced that the law would be tightened so that about one third of all this type of property would be required to be "licensed", whereby local authorities could impose stringent safety conditions and refuse those with relevant convictions. It has taken a long time to get the message through.

Throughout the period 2006-18, the numbers of people renting from private landlords has increased dramatically. For the first time for several generations, from 2014, more people were renting from private landlords than had social tenancies, with many small landlords renting out properties. Indeed, as many as 40% of properties acquired under the right to buy have been turned into private lets in this period. Meanwhile, nationally the overall level of rent increases in the private market between 2012 and 2017 was 11%; much higher than the average rise in wages. It's not surprising therefore that the national housing benefit bill for the sector, doubled between 2006 and 2016, from £4.6bl.to £9.3bl., with the ultimate cost borne by the taxpayer. (House of Commons Briefing Paper 03.04.17)

For those without any home at all, this was not an easy time either. We have seen that the squatting movement in the 1970's (and continuing into the mid '80s) provided the backdrop for the formation of the West 11 Housing Co-op. out of which Portobello Housing Co-op. was born. Over the years successive governments had introduced layers of legislation making it more and more difficult to occupy empty property. Finally, in 2012 squatting was declared a criminal offence. The LASPO legislation which slashed the legal aid system, created a new criminal offence of occupying a residential property; giving the police an immediate power of arrest and the occupier liable to a fine of up to £5,000 and/or imprisonment for up to 6 months. It was widely seen as a pernicious move, doing nothing to tackle either the shortage of housing supply or the prevalence of empty properties. Commercial premises remain excluded despite calls for an extension to that sector too.

Following the implementation of the Human Rights Act 1998, at the beginning of this century, there had been few hallmark court cases in the field of housing. However, at the turn of 2011, the Supreme Court examined two separate cases (*Manchester City Council –v- Pinnock and London Borough of Hounslow –v- Powell)*, both concerning possession of tenancies. The combined effect of the decisions was that (in respect of public sector tenancies at least), the courts could examine whether the commencement of proceedings against an individual was justified having regard to their human rights. As this examination could include all matters right up to the final hearing, the behaviour of the tenant was an issue. However, over the years, Courts have interpreted these rulings narrowly and overall, despite much effort by enthusiastic housing lawyers, the human rights legislation has given little protection from eviction.

During this period, the continuation of sales to council tenants under the right to buy, an increase in housing association disposals and the lack of investment in new stock for letting has resulted in a major problem of housing supply. The Local Government Association reports (13.11.17) that between 2012 and 2017, the difference between Council tenancies lost and the replacements provided, created a shortfall which would have housed 160,000 people. This is confirmed by government figures which showed in March 2017, local authorities owned almost 2 million homes less than in 1994. In contrast between 2014-17, there was a 25 per cent increase in the numbers of families in temporary accommodation in London (including an estimated 100,000 children) (see DCLG homelessness statistics 2017). Many have drawn a link between the two sets of figures. There is also a link between the volume of homelessness and the lack of security of tenure in the private rented sector. Since 2015, roughly one third of all homeless acceptances by local councils, have been due to "no-fault" evictions by private landlords, made possible by the short term lettings introduced in 1988. These figures have quadrupled since 2009 and now represent the largest single reason for homelessness presentation (Local Government Association Report, July 2017).

In an attempt to slow the increase in numbers presenting as homeless, in 2017, the Government adopted a private member's bill going through Parliament. As far back as 2002 the concept of "homelessness prevention" had been identified, but the legislative provisions were without clout and generally unenforceable by the homeless person. The core element is that a local council takes steps to ensure that a person does not cease to have accommodation available for them. The two new measures in the "Homelessness Reduction Act 2017" are:-

- A duty to take steps, without delay, to prevent homelessness, to anyone who is threatened with homelessness within 56 days;
- A duty to all those who are homeless (including those who wouldn't have priority need for re-housing or who may have made themselves intentionally homeless) to give help to end their homelessness.

In order to implement these changes, local authorities have been given £72.7 million for the first three years from commencement in April 2018. It remains to be seen what practical advantages will emerge, but none of it will have any effect on the overall housing shortage, high market rents for private tenants or their lack of security.

Recent Local Events

Politics

In spring 2016, the then Prime minster, David Cameron, called a referendum on whether the U.K. should continue to be a member of the European Union. The vote, on the 23rd of June 2016, was slightly in favour of departing. In Kensington, 68.7% of votes cast were to remain, reflecting the cosmopolitan nature of the area. Negotiations continue at the time of writing and one of the outstanding issues are the rights of those current European Union nationals living in the UK; of which a large number live in the borough. Following the result, Mr Cameron resigned and was replaced by Theresa May who herself called a snap election in the late spring of 2017. This resulted in a no overall majority in the Commons and was widely seen as a mistake. However the most dramatic result came in Kensington. Some 24 hours after the polls had closed and after three recounts, Ms. Emma Dent Coad, a local Labour councillor from North Kensington, was declared elected with a majority of 20 (now the lowest in the U.K.). The swing from Conservative to Labour was over 11% and it was now the most marginal seat in the Country. The decision to leave the E.U. was thought to have had a significant effect on the result. Just five days later, the world of the newly elected MP and the worlds of everybody in North Kensington, would be turned upsides down.

Grenfell Tower

Between 2008 and 2012, plans were developed to transform the extreme south eastern edge of the Lancaster West Estate in North Kensington. As we have seen, this sprawling estate, built in the1970s, housed upwards of 1,000 people and in the '80s had been the subject of legal controversies over infestations and the presence of asbestos. This time the Council wanted to completely transform the "Latimer Triangle" as it was known, by building a 1200 pupil "academy" school and multi-use Leisure Centre – both within meters of the base of the existing Grenfell Tower. The work commenced in 2012, the school was opened in 2014 and the Leisure Centre followed early in 2015, at a total cost of £29 million. In parallel, a scheme of refurbishment works to Grenfell Tower was started in 2015, with responsibility devolved to the Tenants Management Organisation. By January 2016, the Tower Residents' Group had cause to deliver a petition to the landlord, complaining of improper workmanship and again raising concerns on its website as to the adequacy of the means of escape in case of fire. External works included the replacement of windows (none of the flats had access to a balcony) and the insertion of "sandwich" cladding completely throughout all the sides of the building. These external works were completed in the summer of 2016 (cost £2.6 million), the majority of residents concluding that they were mostly, "cosmetic"; designed to blend in with the new school and leisure centre developments and to increase property prices generally in the area.

On the early morning of Wednesday, the 14th June 2017, it is estimated that there were 500 people in the Tower. At 00.54 am, the first call was made to the emergency services, identifying a fire outbreak in a lower floor (thought to be an electrical wiring fault in a fridge freezer). The fire took hold rapidly and ferociously spread up the outside of all four sides of the building, trapping many, particularly on the upper floors, with acrid smoke pouring into the single stairwell preventing escape. A senior fire prevention officer commented that he had seen plumes of flame travel to the top of the building "within 30 seconds" and one of the 250 fire-fighters attending described the scene as "like a war zone" (Evening Standard 15.06.17). The fire burnt for 24 hours after which none of the flats remained habitable; the vast majority of tenants' goods and possessions had been destroyed. Over 60 people were rescued trapped in their homes; 78 people were immediately taken to hospital and we now know that 71 people died; the search for bodies having taken a long time. The vast majority of the deceased and of those who survived were non-U.K. Nationals.

13. Grenfell Tower 2 (August 2017) Michael O'Dwyer

The immediate reaction of the Royal Borough of Kensington and Chelsea (RBKC) was to treat the matter as a minor incident, not allocating extra resources or taking emergency action, attracting criticism for being inept and wholly inadequate. The local community and donors far and wide reacted by urgently giving food, clothes and support to the survivors and families of the bereaved. The generosity was overwhelming and for some time it was of critical assistance.

In August 2017, the government set up a "Task Force" of local government officials, to take over the running of the disaster from RBKC. Its initial report (31.10.2017) states as follows:

"RBKC failed its community on the night of June 14th and in the weeks following. We have heard that RBKC was distant from its residents; highly traditional in its operational behaviours; limited in its understanding of collaborative working and insular, despite cross borough agreements and with a deficit in its understanding of modern public service delivery."

The re-housing of the homeless survivors has been a tortuous business. More than three months from the fire there were 150 households still living in hotels and by the beginning of 2018 sixty-six households are still in emergency accommodation. This demonstrates a continuing mistrust between the victims and the local authority.

The Government quickly announced a Public Inquiry (effectively freezing inquests into individual deaths). Immediately there was criticism both of the scope (omission of any consideration of tenants' legal rights) and of composition of the Panel (which lacked community representation). In September 2017 the Inquiry held an inaugural 45 minute session, after which it retreated into "administrative mode" following which its substantive proceedings commenced in May 2018. It is expected to last for at least a year. In parallel, the national Equality and Human Rights Commission announced in December 2017 that it would be carrying out an investigation as to the role of the State (i.e. both local and central Government) in the tragedy.

As regards legal help for the survivors and their families, the Law Centre was physically located adjacent to the tragedy. As one newspaper reported "North Kensington Law Centre is based in a vast subterranean bunker beneath the Lancaster West housing estate in West London. The doors at the rear of the building are a few feet from the charred remains of

Grenfell Tower" (Guardian 24.07.2017). Immediately after the fire, a local community centre was converted into a makeshift office where help was given on a variety of social welfare legal matters, from bereavement to benefits. Despite vicious cuts in legal aid, the call for volunteers was met robustly, rotas were drawn up with free advice and assistance delivered without restrictions. This continues.

As regards the law itself, there was speculation as to a remedy, from the outset. A retired, senior North Kensington Councillor wrote to the press within weeks of the fire: "I cannot be the only one who, since the Grenfell fire, wonders whether a successful group action on housing disrepair and safety issues might have been possible if these legal aid cuts had not happened." (Mr. S. Hoier, Evening Standard 06.07.17). One person who was not prepared to speculate any further was Karen Buck, M.P. for the adjoining constituency of Westminster North. She had identified that under existing legislation, tenants could do nothing to enforce safety defects in their homes; nor any other defect which caused the property to be "unfit for human habitation". Ms. Buck introduced a private member's bill into Parliament, shortly after the fire, which will give tenants a cause of action to put things right. It is estimated to cover approximately 1 million homes in England and Wales and it will cover matters including fire precautions. Optimistically, in January 2018, the Government "adopted" the Bill which may mean that it will become law sometime in 2019.

Not waiting for the outcome of the Public Inquiry, the Government took steps to address the immediate danger in similar buildings. It is already clear that there are major errors in the Statutory Building Regulations hitherto used in major constructions; a formal review was commenced in August 2017 with results awaited. Further, urgent inspections took place on the nature of cladding to the outside of multi-story buildings, both in the public and private sectors. Emergency guidance was issued in September 2017, including the recommendation that some cladding should be replaced. Of those buildings identified for cladding replacement, at 18.01.2018, out of 160 a total of 3 had been completed and it looks like there will be many disputes before matters are settled.

As a postscript to all this, in January 2018, the "KCTMO" returned to Kensington & Chelsea Council all the properties which it had been managing since 1996 – except, that is, the tenancies in Grenfell Tower, all of which had been completely destroyed.

The changing face of Housing Associations

The Murchison Estate development had caused the demise in 2011 of the Kensington Housing Trust and its assimilation into the group "Catalyst" which took over ownership of all the 530 properties. Between 2012 and 2017 phase one of the development was completed resulting in 150 new homes for sale. Phase 2 started in autumn 2017 and this is expected to produce 330 homes for full or partial sale. There is no defined information as to what is likely to happen to the profits of these sales and no certainty that the remaining social tenants on the estate will benefit. In the middle of the estate is the "Venture Community Centre". Established in 1960 (with the oldest adventure playground in the U.K.) it provides a vibrant range of community events for all ages and is used by all ethnic groups in the area. It is likely to be relocated outside the estate (losing much of its local resonance) as the land it stands on has become too valuable. Adjoining the estate is the "Wornington College" which has been a local further education resource since the 1950s. Given that the ward in which it is located (Golborne) suffers one of the highest levels of deprivation in London (68% of adults not in full time employment at the last Census) it s desperately needed. However, RBKC bought the freehold in 2017 and it is feared that this will become part of the "multi tenure mix" in due course.

In a similar vein, in mid 2017, Notting Hill Housing (it used to be the Notting Hill Housing Trust but the "Trust" seems to have been dropped) announced its intention to cease trading in its own right and to amalgamate its 32,000 properties, with another social landlord, "Genesis", thus doubling the stock. The prospects for occupying low cost social housing in the local area would appear to be minimal. In the past five years, both Notting Hill and Genesis have sold off 800 properties and converted 1322 homes to charge higher rents (47% more for a two bedroom flat than the previous social rent) (Guardian 11.01.2018). Residents are saying that they face more remote management and a domination of commercial interests. Ultimately there is a fear that all the stock in Kensington will be sold for profit, with the loss of social housing units, resulting in a form of "social cleansing" and a changed demography in a hitherto diverse area.

Why has the area lost its two iconic and historical housing associations? One major cause must be the lack of proper regulation. From 1964, for 44 years, housing associations were regulated (and funded) by the Housing Corporation, which had a vigorously active evaluation and monitoring system. It was generally agreed to be both efficient and fair, if a little remote. In 2008, the Government abolished the Corporation and established the "Tenants' Services Authority" (TSA) to regulate delivery of services and "Homes & Communities Agency" (HCA) to regulate financial management and control. In 2012 the TSA was abolished and merged with the HCA and it was declared that there was to be "light touch" regulation where intervention would happen only when tenants would suffer a 'serious detriment'. In 2016, the HCA was itself split into two wings, one financial and one general and in 2018 there is a proposal that it change its name again, to "Homes England". Within this system of "musical chairs", there is very little evidence that serious oversight into standards of service delivery is taking place. Nor is there transparency in any due diligence investigations into mergers and acquisitions between large housing associations, such as those lost to North Kensington. Meanwhile what were once charitable, community institutions are turning into commercial entities.

The Co-op Today

The Co-op is still run by its General Meeting of members, which takes place alternate Fridays from 7pm to 9pm in the Venture Community Centre, W10. Very rarely is there an attendance of less than 70% of the membership and when a member is unable to attend, he or she is expected to send apologies. The Co-op still has no employees but it does commission services such as bookkeeping, financial analysis, banking and insurance matters. Building services are provided after a tendering process, often in conjunction with a consultant surveyor. The Annual General Meeting is the most formal session of the year. On special notice the yearly accounts are inspected, approved and submitted to the regulator set out previously. It is also the venue for the annual election of officers. There are a multiplicity of jobs (which regularly change hands over the years, as the aim is for everyone to play a part in the running of the Co-op). Here are some of the leading posts:

Minutes Secretary

As the General Meeting is the fundamental decision making body, all matters such as finance; repairs; rent payments; maintenance; short life; or external relations, have to be made, approved, altered and/or actioned through it. It is therefore vital to have a comprehensive record of proceedings, this being the responsibility of the Minutes Secretary who produces a draft of the record and circulates to all members (as there will be action points, for work to be carried out. The next

GM corrects any inaccuracies; the Chair signs an approved copy which goes to the Secretary for filing.

The Secretary

This is the post which looks after the legal formalities of the Co-op. Jim McIntyre has been doing the job since 1997 and he reports that the essential ingredients are to keep the records of vital Co-op documents together with responsibility for processing the Annual Accounts (after which, he is responsible for completing the "Annual Return" to the regulator). Overall, he feels that sometimes he is not given enough space in GMs to cover these items adequately but he is content to continue doing the job.

The Chairperson

Simon Morrissey holds this post and has done since 2008. He summarises the ingredients of the job as chairing the fortnightly meetings; making sure that Co-op business is completed; that regulatory requirements are implemented; being a point of contact for outside bodies and being the face of PHC. He summarises the challenges, as follows:

"Maintaining order at GMs; maintaining forward momentum on issues with ongoing obligations and requirements; representing PHC in the constantly shifting landscape that is social housing in 21st Century London."

There are many other Officers, who look after matters including maintenance, insurance, short-life, correspondence-receipt and membership.

The Co-op has always been a self-help organisation. Given its small size and the amount of work needed to be done, each member has been expected to take an active part, not just by attending meetings but also by carrying out tasks needed to keep the Co-op going. Not only is this set out in the governing

Rules, but also it is recognised in the Allocation process for both short-life and permanent properties. The experience of two of the "younger" Co-op members, serves to illustrate this.

Isobel joined the Co-op in June 2008 after having attended meetings for some time. Very soon after, she was housed in short-life accommodation in W11. From the outset Isobel took a keen interest in the task of minute-taking, initially as deputy officer, then with responsibility for minutes' distribution. In 2016, she was elected as deputy membership secretary, taking on the role as full membership secretary the following year. She now also holds the post of "policy records-keeper".

Rosie Lowe was born into the Co-op. Her family home is one of the permanent property tenancies, which is where she grew up. Her first memory of the Co-op was being taken to a General Meeting in a community centre (this would have been in Kensal, W10) aged about 5 or 6 (she says she found it boring). Rosie remembers the Co-op's 25th birthday celebrations in 2004, "Mum and I went on a barge trip with others down the local canal to Camden, and it was fun! Around that time, I remember there was a party in the evening, with live music and lots of people (I was13 years old). I knew then that the Co-op was important." Rosie joined the Co-op in March 2012 after having attended the preliminary meetings and in 2014 was elected short-life officer. Finally, after 22 years living with Mum, Rosie moved into short life accommodation in All Saints Road, W11, in October 2014. Continuing as short-life officer, she began to attend maintenance committee meetings in 2016 and is currently the Co-op's representative on a major refurbishment. In February 2018, Rosie was allocated to one of the Co-op's permanent tenancies.

A Forty Year Housing Legacy

In some ways, access to housing today is not dissimilar to that facing the founders of Portobello Housing Co-op. some forty years ago. In 2017, 85% of Councils nationally declared that they had, "difficulty" in housing single people aged in their twenties (same age as the PHC founders). In North Kensington, the private rented sector is still a significant source of housing (though pricey). The average rent for a one bed roomed flat in or around Ladbroke Grove W10/W11 – at September 2017 – was £1,452 per calendar month). Single people are still excluded from a right to be housed if homeless and there continues to be lots of empty property in the area; residential squatting has been outlawed whereas short-life groups (including Co-ops) have utilized unused units under licence, for many years now. However, as regards North Kensington, there are three matters which have changed life dramatically:

1. **Housing shortage and the Right to Buy.**

   There has never been an "over-supply" of Council housing in the area but what there was has been diminished over the years. Nationally, sales to Council tenants (introduced in 1980) are estimated to have topped 1.8million and are continuing at approximately 22,000 each year. Since 2012, increased discounts for purchasers (amounting to an average of an additional 20%) have led to a four-fold increase in sales applications (Local Government Association, 02.2018). Given that Councils are only allowed to keep one third of receipts and not allowed to borrow to make up the shortfall, replacement accommodation units have not been introduced leading to a decrease in volume and less housing options for those in need.

2. Loss of Security since 1988

The Housing Act 1988 abolished long term protection from eviction in the private rented sector and ended any effective rent control. Nowadays, privately renting is the second largest tenure in the U.K., after owner occupation and the numbers of 25-34 year olds renting has doubled since 2005 (English Housing Survey 2017). The lack of security has a knock-on effect when it comes to homelessness. In the year to 2016, about one third of homelessness applications were due to landlords obtaining "automatic" possession orders (and 4 out of 5 were in London). In July 2017, in bringing these figures out, the Joseph Roundtree Foundation commented that in 2015, there were 10,000 more private sector evictions than in 2003. As regards the cost of renting, we have seen that not only has the housing benefit bill doubled over 10 years, but that someone wanting to live in Ladbroke Grove today would have to find some £17,000 each year to rent a one bed roomed flat.

3. Loss of Housing Charities

One of the governing objects for charities has been the "relief of poverty" and that was the objective of the area's two largest housing associations, Kensington Housing Trust and Notting Hill Housing Trust for many decades, since at least the 1970s. Both organisations pursued vigorous acquisition campaigns, seeking out the most dilapidated property; acquiring for refurbishment (with public money) and letting it to the most deserving. During this time, governments gradually withdrew funding and tenant security was lost. Regulation became an increasingly ineffective "hotchpotch". The recent changes in both organisations has led to speculation that their successors will be more commercially orientated, less community based and more remote from their tenants.

Looking to the Future

In March 2017 the Co-op adopted a paper which proposed a "Root & Branch" examination of four crucial areas of Co-op life:

- Existing policies, procedures and practices
- Future demography of members
- The physical state and nature of the Co-op's stock
- The use of financial resources

Shortly thereafter, each heading was broken down and put to the membership for prioritisation of discussion and decision, categorising short, medium and long term. The process is ongoing. In the same vein, in September 2016, the Co-op recognised that it would be having its 40th birthday in October 2018. It commissioned a history of the Co-op, from its inception. The author agreed to do the writing whilst an editorial group was convened, comprising present and ex-members. Work began in late 2016. Throughout this time, the Co-op has continued to provide housing for its members through self-help and collective voluntary action. The future is unknown but the history is now written.

APPENDIX 1

A CAUTIONARY TALE IN LONDON CLAY

This large property containing 7 self contained flats, sits on a road lined by mature London plane trees and on top of clay soil. Two of the plane trees were situated outside the front garden, on the highway and within 20 feet of the structure. They were the responsibility of the Highway (and Local) Authority, the Royal Borough of Kensington & Chelsea. By 2001, cracks had begun to appear on the ground floor, both inside the two flats and in the common parts. Damage had been caused both to internal walls/ceilings and to exterior brickwork. Subsidence causing damage to the structure was suspected.

P.H.C. is obliged to have property insurance to protect its assets against damage and therefore in late 2001, a claim was made to its insurance company concerning the ongoing deterioration. The insurance company appointed loss adjusters, who in turn instructed a firm of soil analysts whose report found some root damage to the structure and recommended further monitoring. This report was sent to the Co-op but unfortunately never considered at a General Meeting as it was received by a firm of managing agents who misunderstood their brief, failing to pass on to the Co-op, that and similar communications over the following two years.

Finally, in February 2005, a letter was received at the General Meeting, from a firm of consulting engineers (whom nobody had ever heard of) asking for the Co-op's authority to prepare a schedule of "works" (not defined); for delegated authority to decide on contractors and generally to act on the Co-op's behalf. No details were sent regarding the results of monitoring the structure over the previous two years. The General Meeting felt that the firm of managing agents (originally appointed in 1998 to carry out and record rent collection) had exceeded their brief by holding communications regarding subsidence and they were relieved of their duties. Meanwhile the Co-op had to find out what had been happening.

The summer of 2005 saw vigorous attempts to obtain information. The letter of February was challenged and the author was required to set out authority for the wide ranging set of requests. The loss adjusters were asked for details of the claim, their reaction and practicalities of any works to be carried out. The Co-op appointed a dedicated representative officer who was immediately contacted by both the soil engineers requesting access to carry out investigative works involving excavating bore holes and a drain company who wanted to run CCTV trials. All this without any thought for the tenants at the property. To compound matters, the Co-op's officer was contacted by a firm of solicitors, appointed by the insurance company to recover anything paid out as a result of the claim, with no discussion of where this would leave the Co-op.

Completely out of the blue and without any prior consultation, in late summer 2005, the tenants at the property were presented with a schedule of works, bypassing the Co-op's General Meeting and without any reference to the overall state of the structure of the building. The Co-op became increasingly angry at all these various entities taking action without any accountability and without any thought as to the rights of occupiers. None of the correspondence sent earlier in the summer of 2005 had been answered and so the General Meeting resolved not to agree to any further investigative works at the property unless and until a comprehensive report had been delivered, dealing with all aspects of the state of the building. This was confirmed by letter, but it would not be until April 2006 that any reply was forthcoming.

The reply in April 2006, from the consulting engineers, did not include a comprehensive report on the structure but did dismiss (without explanation) any need for underpinning of the building's foundations. In parallel, the Co-op discovered that these engineers had written to various building contractors inviting tenders for the works which had been sent out the previous August. This was the final straw for the Co-op which concluded there had been:

- No consultation on the specification for works, nor any timetable
- No consultation on the proposed firms of contractors selected to tender
- No assurances as to the practicalities for disturbance and/or displacement of tenants
- No assurances as to liability cover within the insurance policy, particularly with regard to payment for works and for ongoing damage.

These matters struck at the heart of the Co-op's founding ethos, the fundamental of self-determination and collective control over property ownership, along with the primacy of tenants' rights. The worry was that the insurance company was "cost cutting" as the proposed works were cosmetic only and would not address the underlying problem. It decided that it had to take radical, swift action and therefore a firm of independent structural engineers was instructed to review the files; inspect the premises and provide recommendations. The report was issued in July 2006 and it found:

- The Plane trees in the clay soil would be having an effect on movement of the structure
- It would be premature to commence repair works until further and more extensive monitoring had taken place
- Need for underpinning to be evaluated after further monitoring
- Whatever the works, the claim should be left open for a number of years to abide future events.

Following submission of the report to the insurance representatives, it was agreed that further monitoring would take place. After initial results, the Co-op's expert again reported in October 2006, indicating that whereas it would appear that underpinning was necessary, the outcome of tree pruning (known as "pollarding") should be considered, by monitoring structural movement within the building, before any works were to commence.

During the next two years, monitoring continued, when, early in 2008 the Co-op was contacted by the firm of solicitors who had been instructed by the insurance company, to "protect its interests". This was the first contact since 2005. They had instructions to press for the nearby trees to be felled as a solution to the structural movement and if necessary, to take the Highway Authority to Court. The Co-op indicated that that should be a last resort and asked to be kept fully informed.

Meanwhile, tenants in the property, particularly on the ground floor, were experiencing widening cracks to walls and ceilings together with structural movement to the exterior and the common parts. In the absence of any remedial works, correspondence with the insurance loss adjuster and consultant engineer became markedly heated. Finally, at the beginning of 2009 the insurance company agreed to carry out major works to all flats at the property; to large areas of the front elevation and for one side of the building to receive underpinning. For an expert opinion on the sufficiency of the proposals, the Co-op referred back to the independent expert who had reported three years earlier. It was advised that the works were reasonable and sufficient on current known evidence but that major drainage works were also needed.

The rest of the year 2009 saw a series of delays in the preparations. The contractors were approved by the middle of the year but there were major problems with the adjoining party wall award. Meanwhile, it was clear that the majority of the flats would have to be vacated for the duration and that alternative accommodation would have to be found, individual tenants took the lead, alongside the Co-op, in negotiations to make sure no one was out of pocket. Likewise, it was clear that for those not vacating, various rooms would be rendered "void" and that goods and possessions would have to go into storage. Again, Co-op representatives negotiated the practicalities of goods out and back, making sure that there was nil cost to the tenants. Finally, with a start date of February 2010, negotiations took place to establish a detailed protocol for day to day working on site. The eventual agreement included:

- Detailed timetable including the sequence of the 7 flats
- Methods of information exchange and updating
- Overall site management with contact numbers
- Responsible working methods including safety and protection of keys
- Communication including handling complaints

- Responsibilities of tenants to fully co-operate and act reasonably

Work took place between February and July 2010. The average length of time within each flat was 3.5 weeks, though for those in alternative accommodation, it was longer. The front of the building was fully scaffolded for 4.5 months. The cost of the works contract was £63,000 but with re-housing costs, storage, professional fees and on-costs, the final costs would be well over double that. In February 2011, the tenants finally received some compensation for the disruption and disturbance – a basic sum of £300 each for the six months, plus an individual sum for loss of amenities, based on time affected and rent payable. This was in accordance with the policy for major works agreed by the Co-op (finalised in September 2010).

Early in 2011, the Co-op was contacted again by the solicitors acting for the insurance company (for the first time since 2008). They were still interested in taking the Council to Court and for the first time, the word "*subrogation*" was used. This turns out to be a "legal doctrine" whereby an insurance company can conduct litigation by "stepping into the shoes" of the insured, to recover amounts they have paid out and/or to prevent further loss. In this brief contact, the Co-op was confused and again asked the lawyers to report fully. After doing some research into the concept of "*subrogation*", the Co-op was troubled to note the following consequences:

- There was no procedure for the obtaining of authority from the Co-op, to take any steps
- There were no checks as to conflict of interest nor terms of business between Co-op and lawyers
- There was no guarantee of any instructions from the Co-op being acted upon

- The Co-op had no standing in the development of litigation, nor any consent needed for action.

The annual "pollarding" of the nearby trees continued, followed by monitoring of structural movement of the building. By April 2012 further structural damaged had been identified in roughly the same areas as the most acute damage previously. Again shrinkage of the clay soil caused by the imposition of tree roots was declared to be the likely cause and in November of that year, a further schedule of works was drawn up (but not acted upon). During this time, the drainage works (which had been delayed for over two years) were finally carried out. The tenants' increasing concerns about new movement in the building were rather overtaken by a contact in October 2014 from the insurance company's solicitors informing that

- County Court proceedings had been issued in April 2011, in the Co-op's name, against the Royal Borough of Kensington & Chelsea – without any notification for 3 years
- The Court action had been then conducted, including the receipt of a defence, incurring Court costs and all other procedural matters – without any notification
- Negotiations between insurance and the Council had taken place – without any notification to the Co-op or request for instructions
- The Court action had been "frozen" for negotiations but that time was rapidly coming to an end.

The Co-op's concerns about "*subrogation*" had come to fruition. An urgent request was made for all documentation, initially only a Court bundle was supplied and after complaint threats, the full documentation was delivered in February 2015. Over a period of 10 years there had been large amounts of correspondence with the Council none of which had been disclosed to the Co-op. There were 187 sheets of correspondence and an equal amount of email traffic. In the ten years since 2005, the Co-op had been contacted a total of three times by the solicitors acting on behalf of the insurance company.

Following this shock and after obtaining confirmation that it would receive a full indemnity from the insurance company, the Co-op became closely involved in the proceedings which were soon to be resolved in that the Council, as Highway Authority, agreed to fell the tree nearest to the property. This was carried out on the 25th March 2015, following which a further period of monitoring took place to confirm stabilisation. Finally, in the second half of 2016, the defects first identified some four years earlier were updated and as there had been stabilisation, a further schedule of works was produced. This again would involve the tenants of the ground floor vacating into alternative accommodation and so the procedure used in 2010 was applied again. Works were carried out early in 2017. The insurance Company continues to attempt to recover its costs from Royal Borough of Kensington & Chelsea.

This process has taken some 16 years and it's not surprising that the tenants at 68, St. Marks Road have been exhausted by it. However, they remain satisfied that they have procured the best outcome both for themselves and for the whole building as the Co-op's asset for the future. It demonstrates the power of collective and determined strength.

APPENDIX 2

ROLL OF HONOUR

Congratulations to all the 145 members and ex-members of the Co-op

who have contributed to its continued existence

and in particular, to those who are no longer with us:

Connor Lynch

"Bud" Abbot

Barry Jennings

Robert "Bucky" Hartnet

Terence Green

Jeremy Green

John Studholme

Payley O'Connor

Simon Pinder

14. Pioneers (1980s)

Lightning Source UK Ltd.
Milton Keynes UK
UKHW02f0140251018
331137UK00001B/3/P

9 781786 233400